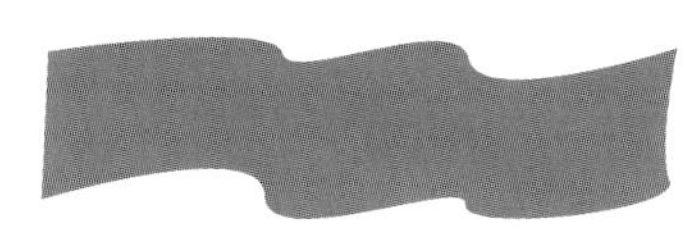

Germany

MIKE HIRST

WAYLAND

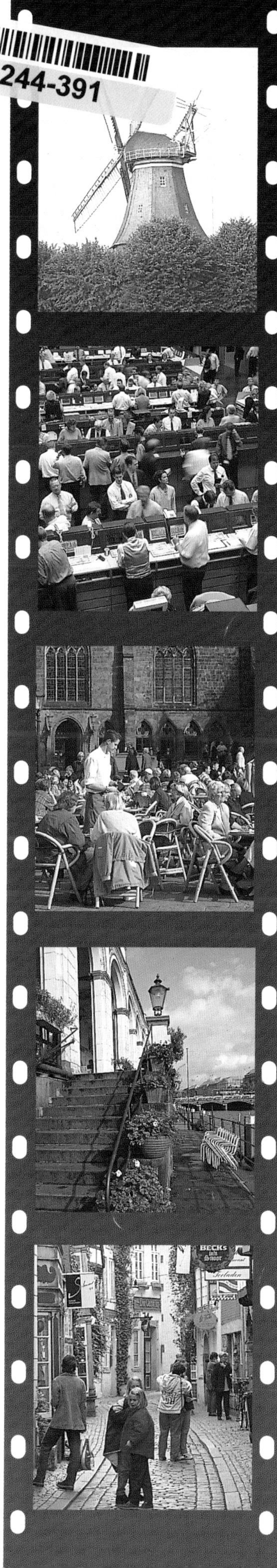

Brazil • China • France
Germany • India • Jamaica • Japan
Kenya • Nigeria • South Africa

The people you are about to meet live in a village in Germany called Bergshausen. Like any country, Germany has many different types of lifestyles. People live in towns and cities as well as in the countryside.

Cover: Moritz, Lisa and some friends get ready for a game of croquet.
Title page: From top to bottom: An old windmill at Kassel; the stock exchange at Frankfurt; a busy café in Bremen; a canalside in Hamburg; and a shopping street in Bremen.
Contents page: These shoppers are having a rest beside a pig sculpture in Hamburg.
Index: The Parisius family has a picnic lunch near a local river.

All Wayland books encourage children to read and help them improve their literacy.

- ✓ The contents page, page numbers, headings and index help locate specific pieces of information.
- ✓ The glossary reinforces alphabetic knowledge and extends vocabulary.
- ✓ The further information section suggests other books dealing with the same subject.

Series editor: Katie Orchard
Designer: Jean Wheeler
Production controller: Tracy Fewtrell

Picture Acknowledgements: All the photographs in this book were taken by Steve Benbow. The map artwork on page 4 is produced by Peter Bull.

First published in 1999 by
Wayland Publishers Limited
61 Western Road, Hove
East Sussex, BN3 1JD, England

British Library Cataloguing in Publication Data
Hirst, Mike
We come from Germany
1. Germany - Geography - Juvenile literature
2. Germany - Social conditions - 1990- - Juvenile literature
I. Title II. Germany
943'.0879

ISBN 0 7502 2226 3

Typeset by Jean Wheeler, England

Printed and bound by G. Canale & C. S.p.A., Turin

Contents

Welcome to Germany

▲ *From left to right: Moritz's dad Moritz Moritz's mum Lisa, (Moritz's sister)*

Moritz Parisius is nine years old. He lives with his mum, dad and older sister Lisa. They have a dog called Paula and a cat called Söcke. The family lives in a village called Bergshausen, in the middle of Germany. You can see where it is on the map on page 5.

▶ *Germany's place in the world.*

▼ *Germany is a large country, right in the middle of Europe.*

GERMANY

Capital city:	Berlin
Land area:	357,000 square kilometres
Population:	82 million people
Main language:	German
Main religions:	Roman Catholic (in the south) and Protestant (in the north)

The Land and Weather

Germany is right in the middle of Europe. The north of Germany is bordered by the sea, and the land is flat. There are lots of hills in the centre of Germany and in the south there are high mountains.

▲ *A sunny day in the village of Bergshausen.*

▶ *There are some beautiful rivers in southern Germany.*

Around Bergshausen the land is quite hilly. There are fields and woods outside the village.

◀ *During the summer, many Germans go to the beaches in the north.*

The weather in Germany changes from one time of the year to another. Summer is usually warm and sunny. Winter is much colder. There is ice and snow, especially in the high mountains in the south of Germany.

▼ *Moritz and Lisa go for a bicycle ride in the autumn rain.*

Just a few kilometres away from Bergshausen lies the town of Kassel. Most Germans live in large cities or towns, such as Kassel.

▲ *There are many shops and offices in Kassel's busy town centre.*

At Home

In Germany many people rent their homes. In towns and cities most people live in flats instead of houses. The people who live in flats don't have gardens, but some have balconies.

▲ *Each flat has a doorbell and letterbox by the main entrance.*

▶ *In busy towns flats jostle for space with tall office blocks.*

'We come to our local park when we want to play outside.' Sonja (right).

▶ *These old houses in Bergshausen have wooden frames.*

The Parisius family lives in a modern house. Mr and Mrs Parisius do not want their home to harm the environment. They try not to use too much gas and electricity.

▼ *Moritz, Lisa and Paula the dog enjoy watching television in their lounge.*

Like many German families, the Parisius family can afford expensive goods, such as a car, a television and a computer.

▼ *Sometimes Moritz finds some interesting creatures in the garden.*

German Food

Germans enjoy their food, and they are proud of their country's special dishes.

German people buy a lot of their food in supermarkets, but there are still many small shops too. Most neighbourhoods have their own baker and butcher.

▲ *Favourite evening snacks are sausages, dark bread called pumpernickel, and pickled fish called rollmops.*

▶ *Colourful outdoor markets sell fresh fruit and vegetables.*

◀ *Customers choose their own vegetables at the supermarket.*

TENUTA SERENA
CICLA
DEUTSCHER
EISSALAT
Annalisa
UUM COOLED

15

▲ *The Parisius family sits down to a tasty traditional breakfast.*

The Parisius family often have a large breakfast, with boiled eggs, bread and cheese. There is sometimes ham or meat paste too.

Many Germans like to have a cooked meal at lunch time. In towns and cities, hungry office workers crowd into cafés or busy restaurants.

▶ *On warm days, you can have lunch at an outdoor café.*

'People come to my stall for a tasty snack of sausage and bread.' Mr Graf, food stall owner.

BECK's AM MARKT

At Work

Industries making goods such as cars, electrical goods and machinery, provide a lot of jobs in Germany.

▼ *At the stock exchange in Frankfurt, people invest money in German industries.*

'I love to help people. Being a psychiatrist is my dream job.' Moritz's mum.

In Bergshausen, some people work at the farms in the village. Many others work at a large car factory nearby.

Moritz's mum works as a kind of doctor called a psychiatrist. On some days she works in a surgery that is part of the Parisius' home.

◀ *Mr Schmidtt is a pig farmer in Bergshausen.*

At School

German children begin school by going part-time to a nursery called a *kindergarten*. Primary school starts when they are six years old.

▶ *Children crowd on to a bus to be taken to school.*

▼ *These children are hard at work, building a model rocket.*

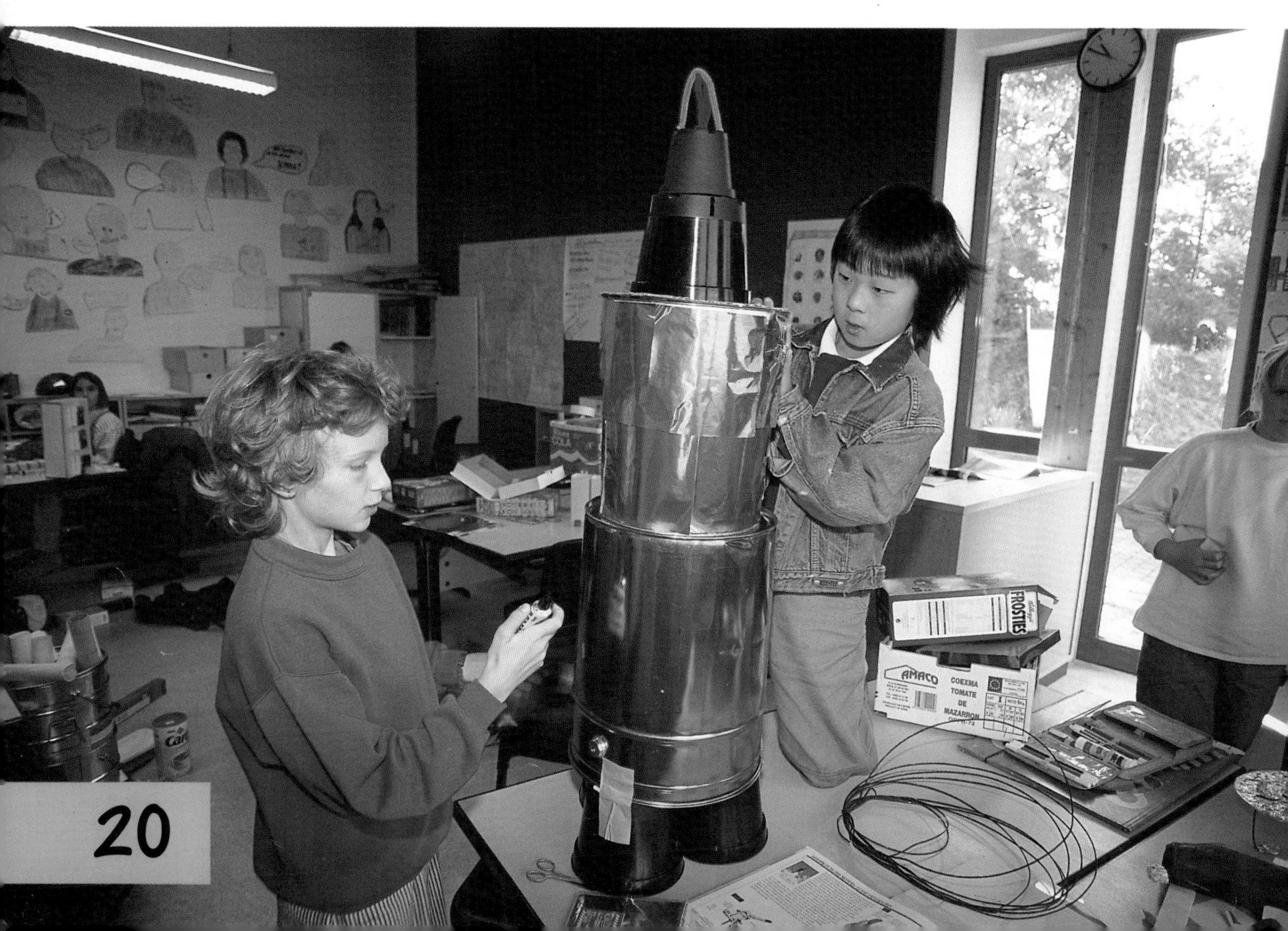

The school day begins at 8 o'clock in the morning. There are lessons all morning, with two short breaks. When lessons finish at 1 o'clock, the children go home in time for lunch.

▲ *Children work in pairs on the school computers.*

There are about 25 boys and girls in Moritz's class.

Moritz has just started at a new school. It is in the nearby town of Kassel and he travels there every day by bus.

Moritz's school is in a brand-new building. There is plenty of modern equipment, and each class has its own computers.

Every afternoon, Moritz has to do some homework.

'I like art and English, but my favourite subject is football!' Moritz.

Free Time

Sports are very popular in Germany, especially football and swimming.

Bergshausen has its own youth club, run by a local church. Children go there to play games such as table tennis.

▲ *Lisa is learning to play the mandolin in her spare time.*

▶ *This girl is learning how to unicycle at a youth club.*

'If the weather's fine, we all go out fishing together.' Moritz.

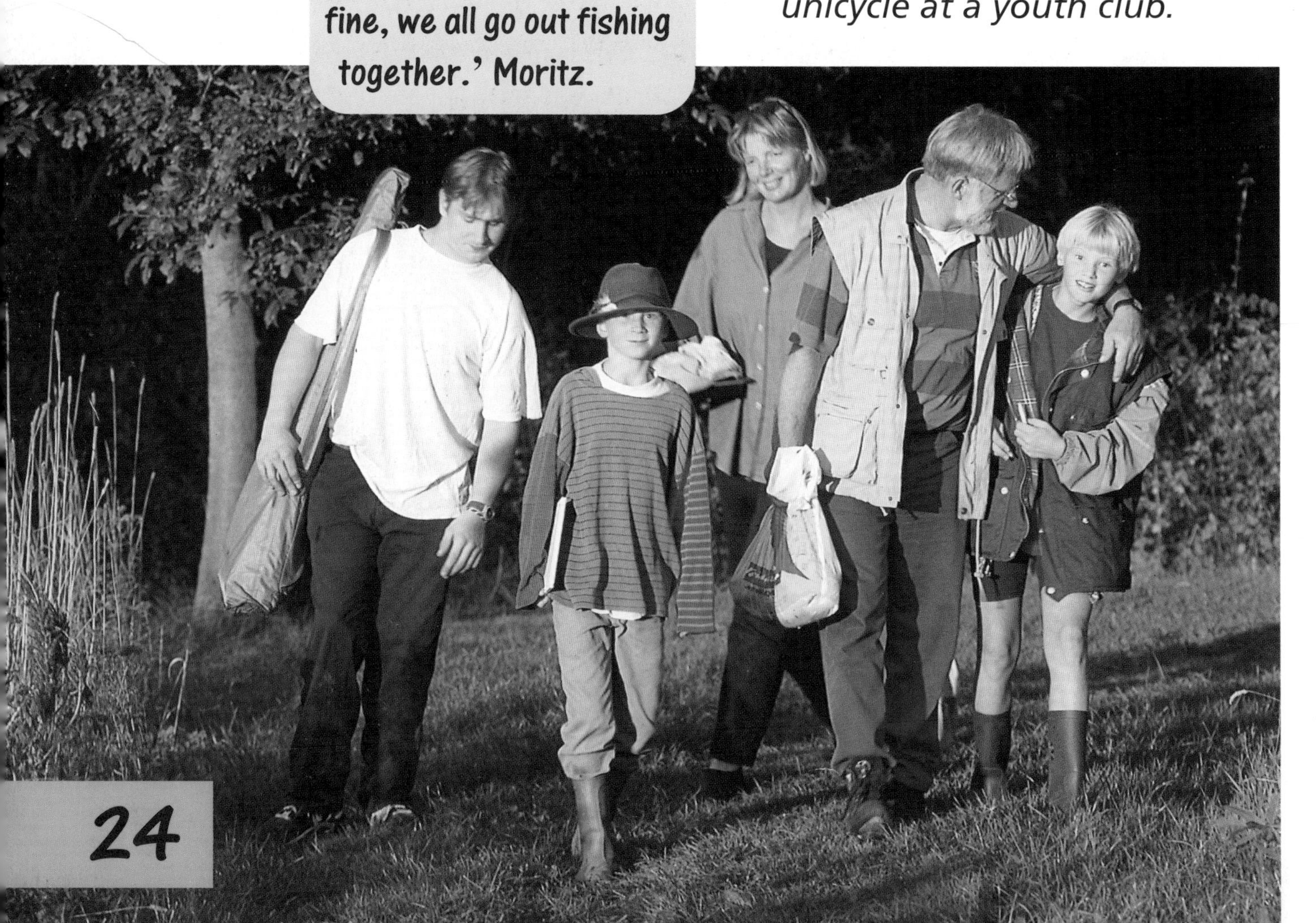

Looking Ahead

Germany is a modern, wealthy country. Its factories make goods such as cars, mobile phones and hi-fi equipment which are sold all over the world.

Many Germans are worried about the harm that cars and industry can do to the environment. They want to stop pollution in towns and cities.

▶ *New buildings shoot up in a city centre.*

BERLINER CITY TOUR
STOP
S

December Biscuits

Moritz and his family like to eat December biscuits on St Nicholas' Day (on 6 December) and at Christmas. They are very easy to make.

▲ *Moritz starts to make the dough.*

You will need:

100 g butter
75 g caster sugar
1 egg
200 g plain flour
half teaspoon mixed spice
half teaspoon ground cinammon
1–2 tablespoons of milk

- First, cream the butter and sugar together in a mixing bowl.

▲ *Moritz's mum and sister use oven gloves to take the biscuits out of the hot oven.*

- Then, separate the egg yolk and beat it into the mixture. Sift in the flour and spices and mix well. Add the milk and knead the mixture into a soft dough.
- Roll out the mixture on a floured board, until it is about 5 mm thick. Cut out star or moon shapes. Brush the top of each shape with the egg white.
- Ask an adult to bake the biscuits for 10–12 minutes at Gas Mark 6/200 °C.

Germany Fact File

Money Facts

◀ German money is the mark, which is divided into 100 pfennings. £1 is worth about 3 marks. Carl Friedrich Gauss, the famous mathematician, can be seen on the 10 mark note.

Famous People

Famous German people include Johann Guttenberg who invented the first-ever printing press, during the fifteenth century and the Brothers Grimm, who wrote Grimm's Fairy Tales. Former Wimbledon champions, Boris Becker and Steffi Graf are both from Germany.

River Facts

Germany has several major rivers, such as the Rhine, the Elbe and the Danube.

The German Flag

▼ The red, black and gold represent a long struggle for a united Germany.

Mountain Facts

The highest mountain is the Zugspitze, in the Alps. It is 2,963 metres high.

The Berlin Wall

After the Second World War, Germany was divided into East Germany and West Germany. In 1961, East Germany's government built a wall through Berlin to stop its people going to West Germany. In 1990 East Germany and West Germany became one country again and the Berlin Wall was torn down. ▼

Car Industry

Germany is famous for producing high quality cars, which are sold all over the world.

Delicatessen

There are many different types of sausage to choose from in Germany, from *bratwurst* to *salami*. ▼

CHAPTER
THE GARDEN
ENVIRONMENT
ONE

Right. *A low water table (a) allows unrestricted root growth which means that the plant will prosper. The shallow depth of unsaturated water offered by a high water table (b) will hinder root penetration and thus restrict the plant's growth.*

SOIL

THE SUCCESS OF ANY GARDEN naturally depends on the growth of its plants. This in turn depends on having a soil which provides the right characteristics to promote strong, healthy growth.

Soil is a living medium, made up of solids, liquid (water) and gas (mainly air), and provides all that is needed for many tiny organisms to prosper. The solid material consists of particles of various sizes, each of which have particular qualities:

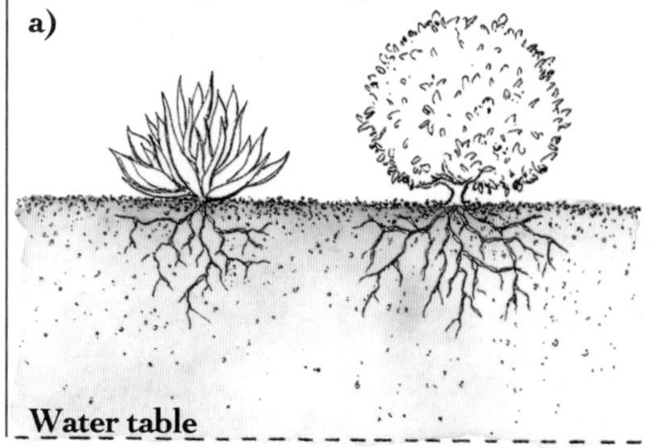

Stones have little to contribute to the soil despite their size. Being totally inert, their only effect is to displace more useful particles, so reducing the volume of soil which plant roots come into contact with.

Sand is the largest of useful particles. Its coarse texture allows comparatively large spaces (pore spaces) between the grains through which water can pass.

The size of particle provides only a small surface area relative to its volume, and as such it can hold only a relatively small amount of nutrients. A soil that has a high proportion of sand, therefore, will be quick to drain but is

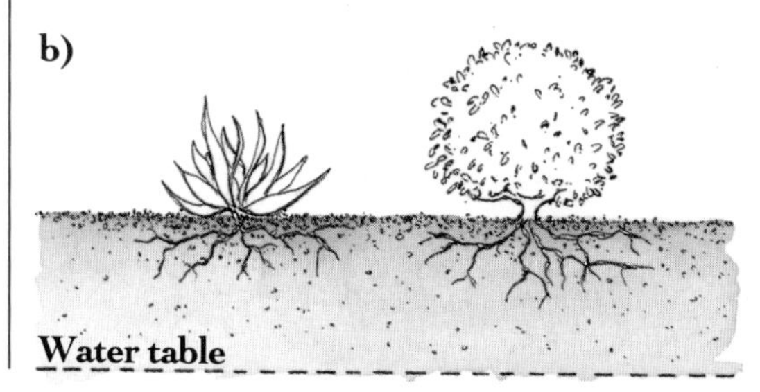

Below right. *The gradual breaking-down of leaves, small twigs, etc, will result in a soil rich in organic matter which here supports a thriving colony of* Cyclamen coum.

***Left.** Nutrients are quickly washed from a sandy soil resulting in poor, weak plant growth. This* Kerria japonica *shows strong sytmptoms with parts of the plant actually dying back.*

likely to be poor. Any nutrients not securely held by the grains of soil will be quickly washed away.

Silt comes between sand and clay in both particle size and water-holding characteristics, although it tends to have properties more closely aligned to those of a clay soil.

Clay is formed from the smallest particles in the soil. Their minute size enables them to lock together tightly, making the passage of water or oxygen very difficult. They have a comparatively large surface area which can hold large quantities of nutrients, but in a so-called 'clay soil' (where clay particles are dominant), root growth is inhibited, making many of the nutrients unavailable to them.

The final solid constituent of soil is **organic matter**, mainly derived from decaying plants. This is broken down by a variety of living organisms – such as earthworms and fungi – to provide nutrients.

An ideal soil is usually considered to be a loam soil; this consists of approximately 50 per cent sand, with the remainder of the soil in roughly equal proportions of silt and clay, and around 5 per cent organic matter. This provides a reasonably free-draining soil with good structure and a high availability of nutrients.

The relative acidity or alkalinity (pH) of a soil is also important. Many lime-hating plants will not tolerate an alkaline soil, and an extremely acid soil will prevent many other plants from establishing. An ideal pH of around 6-6.5 will give a neutral soil suitable for most plants, although a more acid soil is preferred by rhododendrons and similar plants.

__Far right, top.__ Modern drainage systems commonly use perforated plastic pipes which may be either rigid or flexible and come in a variety of lengths. Traditionally short clay pipes 12"-18" (30-45 cm) long were placed end to end leaving a small gap which would be covered by tiles as shown.

__Right.__ The backfilling of a soakaway would begin with a deep layer of large stones or clean hardcore. Above this a thinner layer of small stones would be topped by a filter membrane or upturned turfs to prevent soil washing down into the stones. The final layer would be topsoil, improved as necessary with sharp sand. Such a soakaway should be deep enough to extend beyond any impervious layer in the soil.

__Far right, centre.__ Larger drainage systems are usually constructed on a herringbone layout and laid to a gradual fall — leading to a soakaway or a sump and then on to the main drainage system. Where the soil drains particularly badly a smaller spacing (a) would be used.

__Bottom.__ The backfall around a drainage pipe would be similar to that of a soakaway (above) but using smaller aggregates in the first two layers.

Improving the soil

The addition of organic material in the form of manure, peat or compost will help. This breaks up heavy clay soils making them drain more freely and easier to work; it will also mean easier root penetration which will help to unlock the abundance of nutrients in the soil. With coarse, sandy soils, organic matter will help retain moisture and prevent nutrients being so easily leached or washed out of the soil. Where the depth of topsoil is less than the desired minimum of about 9"/22.5cm, the upper parts of the subsoil layer can be improved

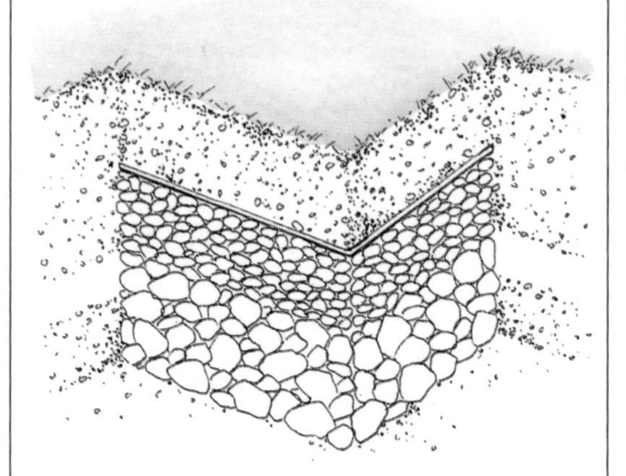

by cultivation and by adding organic material: this provides a deeper root run for the plants.

Altering the drainage capacity of a soil can also help to improve it. Pore spaces between soil particles are filled with either water or air: as the water is removed from the soil system by draining, or by evaporation or plant use, it is replaced by air which provides oxygen to the plant roots. A poorly drained soil will have little space for air and so will be stale and uninhabitable by roots. Because of this, a very shallow water table will reduce the amount of soil available to the plant.

By improving drainage, the effective depth of soil is increased. A better ratio of water to air is created within the soil system, thus allowing better growth.

The simplest form of drainage is the soakaway, a large pit dug at the lowest point in the garden where water collects. This is filled with large stones or clean hardcore, covered with a filter membrane to prevent the stones becoming clogged with soil (upturned turves can

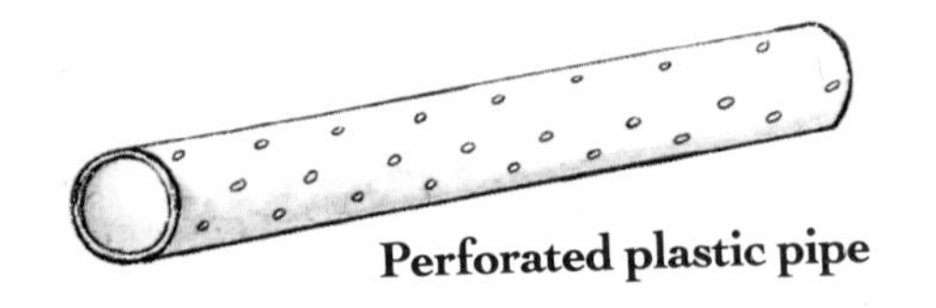

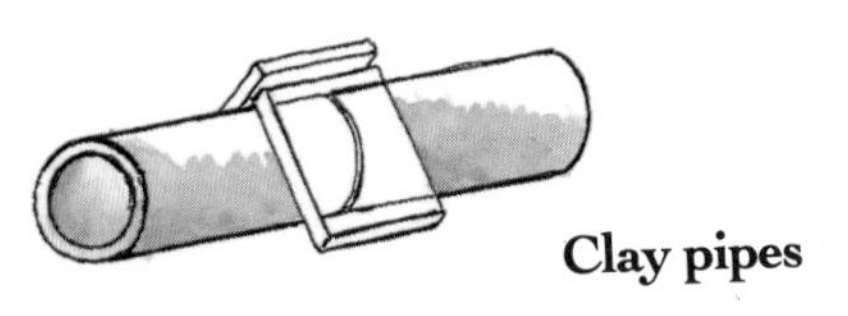

provide an adequate filter in many cases) and covered with top soil. A more complex system would involve the addition of a series of land drains throughout the garden, spaced according to the soil type, which would channel water to the soakaway.

Alternatively, a system of land drains can be connected to the main surface water drainage

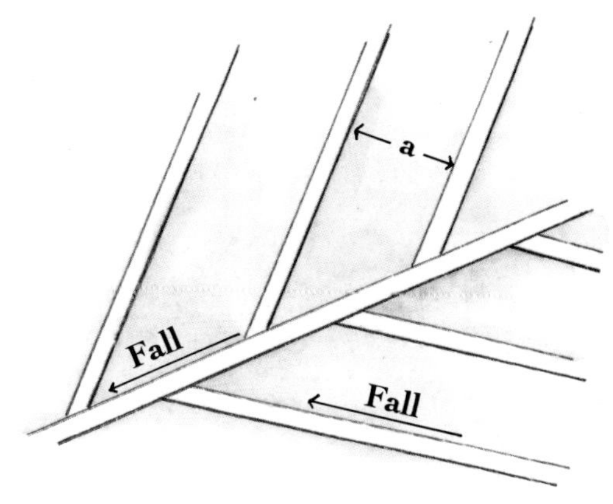

system by means of a sump. This arrests soil particles washed through the system and prevents them from being passed into the main drainage system.

The choice of drainage system used will depend on the site, soil and layout as will their positioning. Detailed advice should be sought

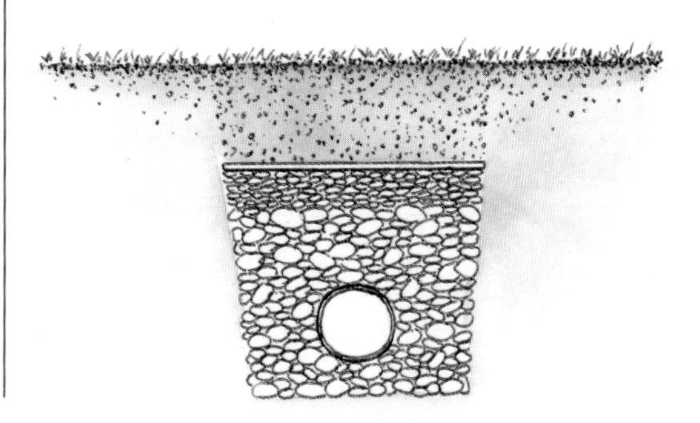

Above. *Tall leafy planting including* Datura *with its pendulous cream flowers and a brightly-coloured parasol lend cool shade in a hot climate while giving the garden its own particular style.*

from garden experts and centres as to which system best suits the situation, and any garden layout must be devised to take account of the drainage system to be installed.

CLIMATE AND MICROCLIMATE

The climate, or macroclimate as it is more correctly known, varies widely from region to region and country to country and is dependent on latitude, prevailing winds, topography and position relative to the sea. How these factors affect the garden — including the effects of solar radiation, temperature, precipitation, air movement and humidity — will quickly help to shape both the design and use of a garden.

If it falls within an area of high rainfall, a garden will no doubt require paved paths around its edges; where there are strong winds, sitting areas will need shelter or positioning in a protected area; in hot, arid climates gardens

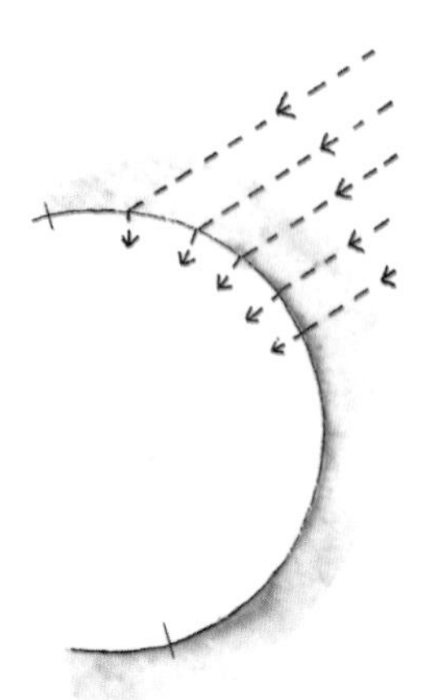

Above. Radiation from the sun is more intense nearer the equator due to the curvature of the earth.

Below. Ground sloped towards the sun will receive a higher intensity of radiation and so warm up more quickly.

will require shade, while further north, maximum exposure to sunshine may be sought.

Such wide variations of climatic conditions makes the selection and siting of plants of paramount importance. As a rule of thumb, it is best to select plants similar to those that do well in comparable conditions in the wild.

Although the macroclimate varies from one place to another, the way it interacts with plants and various structures in a localized area forms a microclimate. The effect may be so localized that a large number of microclimates can be created in even a small garden which has areas which are more, or less, exposed.

Radiation

Plants require quite high levels of radiation to grow successfully, but less than half of the sun's radiation that reaches the earth's atmosphere actually penetrates to the earth's surface. The intensity of radiation is proportional to the angle with which the sun's rays meet the ground, and this depends on both latitude and topography. As the distance from the equator increases, the number of growing days is reduced and the temperature is generally lower. And ground that is sloped towards the

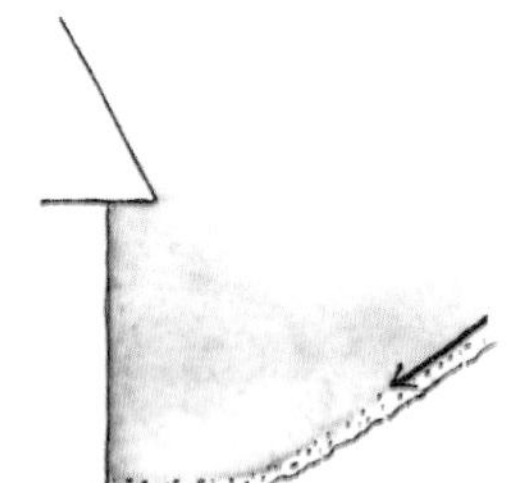

Above. Obstructing the flow of cold air down a slope may create a harmful frost pocket.

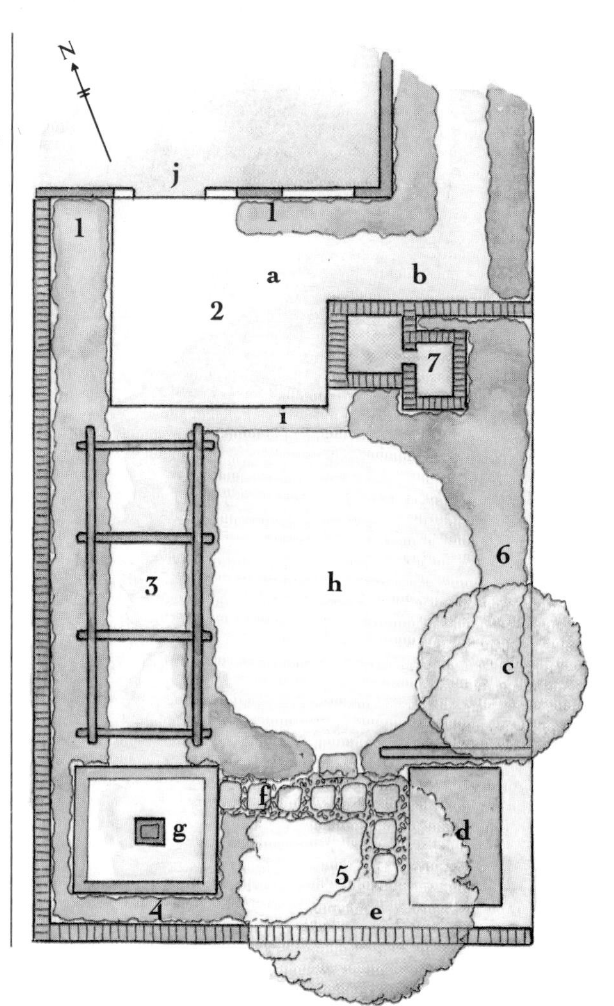

Opposite page, top. Subtropical planting will only thrive in hot humid climates similar to those of its natural habitat.

In a cooler climate, a double glazed conservatory, ***left,*** *will allow the garden to be used over much of the year while providing additional living space. The conservatory should always be style to suit the house.*

Opposite page, bottom. *A wide variety of microclimates can be created in even a small garden as illustrated by this compact design for a European garden.*
Key: a) paved terrace; b) low retaining wall; c) small tree; d) shed screened by trellis; e) large tree; f) stepping stone path; g) statue/sundial on area of paving; h) lawn; i) step up from terrace; j) french windows.
Key to microclimates; (1) Warm south- and southwest-facing borders, backed by walls.
(2) Warm, sunny terrace for tender plants in pots (protected indoors during colder months).
(3) Timber pergola gives light shade and protection from ground frosts.
(4) Dry border area due to rainshadow cast by wall.
(5) Heavily shaded area beneath tree.
(6) Harsh east-facing microclimate — exposed to cold easterly winds and sudden thawing by early morning sun.
(7) Two-tiered pool giving areas for marginal and aquatic plants and cooling the atmosphere.

sun will receive more radiation than level ground or land which slopes away.

Radiation received by the earth during the day is radiated back both during the day and to a greater extent by night. Back radiation can cause such heat losses that harmful ground frosts occur. An insulating mantle of cloud helps to minimise this effect, as do other shields such as trees, which reflect radiation. Ground below trees and larger shrubs is therefore reasonably sheltered and less liable to harmful frosts than a more open position. Where there are no protecting trees or shrubs, a layer of insulating material such as straw may be placed over the more vulnerable plants in the garden when frosts are likely.

Frost pockets can also be a problem. These occur where the path of cold air flowing slowly down a slope is blocked, by a building, for example, and the resulting build-up of cold air saps heat from the ground, encouraging frosts. Where possible, such obstacles should be avoided, allowing an uninterrupted path down which the cold air can flow.

Areas of stone and bricks absorb great quantities of radiation by day, and release it slowly throughout the night. This allows a south-facing wall, for example, to provide a suitable habitat for tender plants even in quite cold climates, as the wall holds even a minimum of warmth.

Wind

In most climates wind is considered a negative force. Although it can help in reducing frost, it can also mean considerably reduced tempera-

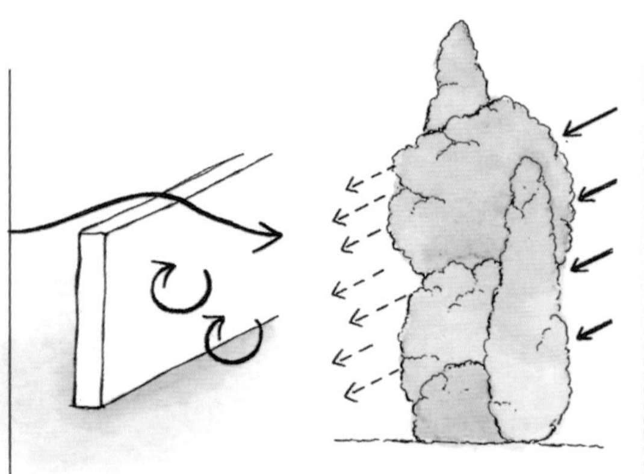

Right. *A solid wall or fence will cause the wind to eddy behind the barrier, resulting in very little reduction in speed and force. A permeable barrier or mixed evergreen and deciduous planting will be far more efficient in filtering the wind.*

tures and possible physical damage by being excessively cold or hot.

The wind characteristics will depend on where it has come from. A wind blowing over a wide expanse of sea is liable to be mild and wet, while that blowing from land is more likely to be dry and possibly very cold in winter, since air cools much more quickly over land, particularly if blowing from the north.

To reduce wind speed in a garden, to protect plants and to give shelter, means erecting some form of deflector. A solid barrier such as a wall is far less effective than might be expected, as the wind merely flows over the top of the wall with no real reduction of speed. A permeable barrier, such as a slatted fence or belt of mixed planting, will be far more effective, with a permeability of around 40 per cent being the ideal. Such a wind-break will filter the wind sufficiently to give a significantly reduced flow over a distance 10-15 times its height.

Reducing the wind speed in one direction can only increase it in another and care must be taken not to bring about harmful build-ups of wind along the surface of a wall or fence. Planting wind-resistant shrubs and climbers alongside walls and fences will help to prevent the windspeed increasing along their length. Windbreaks should also continue right to ground level to avoid funnelling the wind beneath them.

Rainfall and Evaporation

Obviously, little can be done to alter the level of rainfall in the garden, but it is important to avoid the creation of rain shadows. The dense foliage of large shrubs or trees can prevent rain reaching the area beneath it; a structure or building in the path of the main rain-bearing winds will create a comparatively dry area on the leeward side.

In order to survive, a plant must balance its water losses which occur through evaporation, with its supply. While some plants may be naturally adapted to growing in dry areas, with leaves that are either very small or have a waxy surface which prevents water loss, others may require both shade and shelter from the wind. Plants growing in an area where they regularly receive less water than they need will require some form of irrigation, and this could be as simple as using a watering can or hose; or it may be desirable to install a complete irrigation system, consisting of sprinklers or more sophisticated self-regulating systems available from garden equipment stockists, who can also give advice on uses and the installation of such systems. As with an underlying drainage system, this should be planned into the garden at the outset to help prevent problems later.

A mixed planting of conifers and rhododendrons, ***left,*** *privides good wind protection right down to the ground.*

Left. *A lawn edge sprinkler fits unobtrusively into the scene yet provides adequate irrigation for this island bed.*

CHAPTER
DESIGN BASICS
TWO

A BASIC COMPREHENSION of garden design leads to taking better decisions concerning both the retention of existing features and in the creation of any new layout. The principal areas of concern are discussed below.

Balance

Using three dimensional drawings, any design can be reduced to a series of voids and masses which helps to check whether a layout is balanced or not. A garden which is unbalanced, particularly along the main viewing axis (usually from the house), will have an unsettled feel to it. The aim in balancing is to achieve an effect where the sum of the masses on each side of the garden is not too dissimilar from that on the other.

The main masses to be considered are buildings and plants, particularly trees and larger, screening plants. An unsightly building on the boundary of a garden will not only need screening but may also require balancing, as the combined effect of a building with a screening planting will be particularly pronounced. Too many points of interest in a small area of the garden will also lead to imbalance. Each major feature should be given its own space, which will not only give it greater impact, but help the design as a whole.

***Below.** When viewed from the french windows the plants that screen the garage, coupled with the general shape of the plot, could easily unbalance the design. The use of a large tree, bold foliage and a bench to the right of the main viewing axis brings the garden back into balance.*

KEY: a) french windows; b) paved patio; c) large over-hanging shrub; d) bench; e) large bamboo; f) stepping stones; g) reflecting pool; h) statue/ornament; i) pergola with brick piers; j) paving; k) step up; l) timber-decked sitting area; m) screening tree and shrubs; n) garage; o) large tree; p) compost and storage; q) screening shrub.

Strong Lines and Perspective

The intelligent use of perspective has an important role to play in garden design. The human eye can be easily deceived or mislead in

The straight lines of the path and the repetition of metal arches gives great perspective depth to the view, ***left,*** *and draws the onlooker into the garden.*

what is sees, and lincs running along the site (ie away from the house) will tend to lengthen it, while those running across the garden will make it appear wider. The lines could be details in the paving, the sides of a path or even the edges of a lawn; they can all be used to alter the visual shape of a plot.

Whereas in a large garden perspective will be naturally apparent, in a smaller space this may disappear. However, converging lines will help to force a perspective of length, whereas diverging lines will have the opposite, shortening effect. The positioning of features such as paths, pergolas and walls can therefore be used

Left. *A more open but equally lengthening effect is created by this straight gravel path and narrow borders of lavender and bedding plants.*

Above. Alternative panels of insitu concrete and granite setts give textural interest to this bold, sweeping path. The finely cut leaves of bordering geraniums complement the effect.

to great effect, and should be undertaken with care. Careful placing of coarser textures — plants with larger leaves, stones or large paving slabs — near the main view point and fine foliage, pea shingle and smaller unit paving further away will deceive the eye. By giving the eye the necessary visual stimuli — in this case, that things in the distance are smaller — the brain can be led to believe that a true perspective exists.

'Atmospheric perspective' can also be used in this situation, and is best described as a watering down of colour as it recedes into the distance: the same effect that gives mountains their blue-grey colour when viewed from afar. Pastel shades and foliage with a grey or blue hue will bring the feeling of atmospheric perspective into the garden. The opposite foreshortening effect of bright colours applies too, even in a large garden.

Texture

Variety in paving types and leaf size used in the garden will heighten visual interest: everything has a texture, be it in the fine appearance of gravel and closely mown lawn, or the boldness of *Bergenia* leaves and cobbles.

The balance of fine and bold textures — and all the stages in between — is a matter of personal taste, but as a rule the bolder textures of cobbles, large foliage types, etc, should be used sparingly. Larger components used to excess can lead to a disturbing imbalance.

Different effects can be created by blending or contrasting various textures, some of which will be quite marked. Coarse textures contrasted against fine — such as bold foliage types against grass or railway sleepers against gravel — can be used to attract and hold the eye successfully. Smooth and fine surfaces, such as paving, grass and gravel, should normally be

Above. *The tightly clipped foliage of a dwarf box hedge (*Buxus sempervirens *'Suffruticosa') would be considered a fine texture until compared with the closely mown lawn. The strong lines running across the view have a forshortening effect.*

Left. *The fine appearance of gravel acts as an excellent foil for the brick-paved circles and paths and the stylish timber seats. The gravel here has been bonded in resin to give a stable surface which can be washed or brushed clean.*

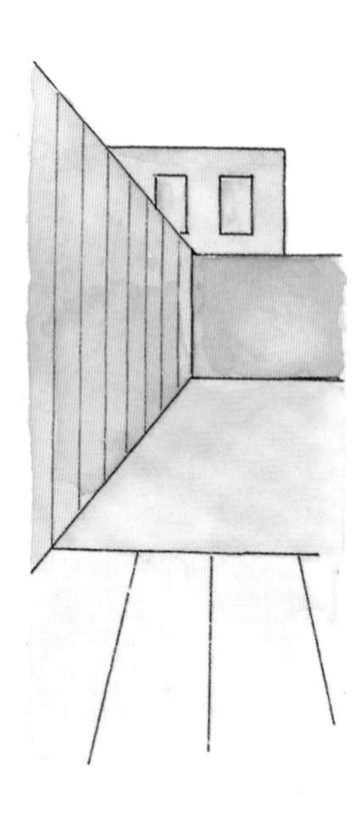

*An ugly building which overlooks the garden from beyond the perimeter (**left**) may be screened just as well by a smaller object or plant placed nearer the viewpoint (**right**) as by a much larger object or plant placed further away (**far right**).*

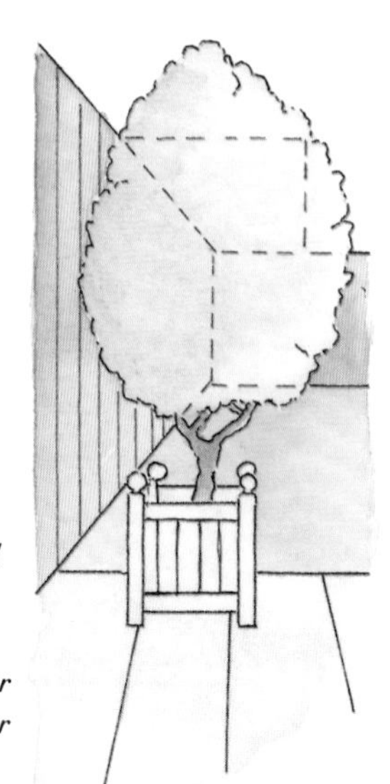

***Right.** The strongly weeping nature of* Betula pendula *'Youngii' (Young's weeping birch) tends to hold the eye down near the ground, a useful ploy when space for screening is limited.*

*The tall bank and planting of rhododendrons (**below**) successfully screens the surroundings and helps to focus the eye on the small informal pool below.*

used as the main surfacing, as they provide an even and unobtrusive background for other, coarser, textures.

Every element used in a garden has to be considered in the context of texture. A paving slab with its smooth surface, for example, would normally be considered a fine texture, but when contrasted with brick or other paving materials, its large size would make it appear coarse. Such anomalies can only add further interest and a case can often be made for breaking the rules.

Framing and Screening

If a garden is fortunate enough to have a pleasant view, this can be incorporated into the overall design, effectively enlarging the garden. Particularly strong and interesting items such as a distant church spire or a large tree can even be framed to form the main focal point of the garden.

Others may wish to screen out or obscure their surroundings. Screening is most commonly provided by planting, fences and walls, although overhead structures also have a part to play. In many small gardens, screens are often placed around the edges of a garden, but an object nearer the onlooker will screen a larger area than one further away. It might therefore be better to bring the screening into the garden in many cases. A large plant in a tub on the terrace might screen as much as a tree placed near the boundary.

If adequate screening is impossible, a strong ground pattern may help to hold the eye within the boundaries. Plants and particularly trees of a weeping nature help, as the eye is liable to follow the line of the tree and so to be returned to ground level.

Just as items beyond the boundaries can be framed, so can objects within the garden. This too can be used to detract from unattractive surroundings.

Intrigue

Visual interest is one of the main goals in designing a small garden and this can be

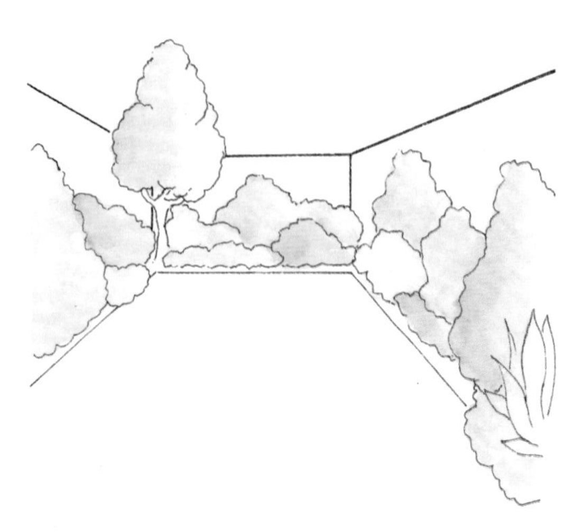

*A very open garden (**left**) holds few surprises and can be taken in almost at a glance. By partly screening an area (**right**) interest is immediately created without losing the feeling of space.*

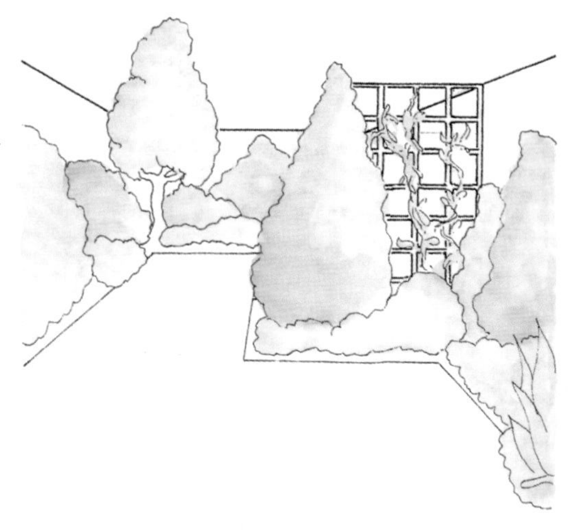

*The peephole through a garden wall (**below**) allows only a restricted view and encourages further exploration.*

***Left.** The bright foliage of massed* Coleus *plants mingle easily together as the colours all come from the limited yellow to red range of the spectrum.*

heightened by creating intrigue. Spacial division, in the form of screens and visual blocks, will accentuate various parts of the garden and so prevent the whole scene being absorbed at once. The scale of division will largely depend on the size of plot, but even a small area hidden from direct view will go a long way towards maximizing interest.

Colour

The use of colour in the garden depends on the quality of light as well as individual hues. Although bright colours stand out, they need a high intensity of light to show the true depth of colour. Pale colours, particularly blues, will tend to be washed out by strong sunlight, so a partly shaded position is better for them. Pastel shades have a receding effect in contrast to bright colours, and in general will combine more easily to form an area over which the eye can flow uninterrupted.

Combining colours satisfactorily is a difficult task. Single borders or even whole gardens can be planned on a single colour theme with, for example, a yellow border which encompasses a

Above. *An elegant white-painted seat makes a commanding focal point.*

A pink grey border ***(opposite page, top)*** *gives a variation of hues that lead the eye gently along the border.*

Opposite page, bottom. *The enormous conifers dominate the house giving it a quaint 'cottegey' appeal.*

full range of flowers from rich golds through lime greens to creamy whites. The flowers would be set against a varied backdrop of green, golden and variegated foliage, with touches of grey to add further depth.

The colour of building and paving materials is just as important as that of plants. Mellow stone colours provide the best foil for plants. Unless it is intended to stand out, timber work should be stained dark although lighter colours will tone down as they weather. Green as a stain, paint or stone colouring should generally be avoided. If an object or structure is to be highlighted, white is often the most appropriate colour as it is bright but also combines well with other hues and shades in the garden.

Materials

The selection of paving and walling types is often a daunting prospect. Choose those which are in keeping with the house — after all, it is the largest and most influential part of the garden setting. Where bricks are to be used they should match the house wherever possible, and when in doubt the simplest materials are likely to be the best. One or two materials used in repetition throughout the design will have a unifying effect, linking the various elements of the garden and holding them together.

The pre-cast concrete paving slab in its vast array of shapes and finishes has been used in the design of many modern gardens. But in smaller

areas, more expensive, high-quality materials, such as natural stone paving, might be a possible alternative.

SCALE AND PROPORTION

The need for scale in a garden is overwhelming, or one element could easily overpower the others, causing visual disturbance. Similarly too many small features cluttered into a large garden give a 'bitty' and confused look. Architectural features such as paving, paths and walls must be in proportion to the house, and the planting should be in scale with both these and the overall design. These rules extend down to the more intricate levels of pattern and texture. Particular skill must be employed if a tiny garden is to be successfully combined with a large multi-storied house.

In most cases where there is space, a large building will need large-scale planting to merge it into the landscape. Comparatively small

Below. *A narrow terrace is overpowered by the house. Widening the paved area and adding planting by the house gives a far more satisfactory result.*

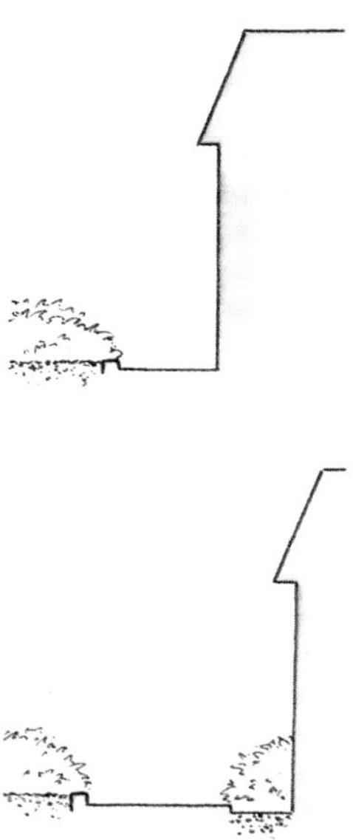

buildings could be dwarfed by a large tree and bold planting, for example, or smaller trees and planting can make it appear larger and more impressive.

One of the most successful ploys in a small garden is to make it appear as the only visible part of a larger estate: mirrors can be used here, apparently opening up whole new vistas and sections of garden. Obscuring the boundaries of a garden with a band of planting and shadows will also immediately disguise its size, making it easier to merge with the house.

The scale of planting not only depends on the size of individual plants, but also on their shape and on the groups in which they are massed. Although of only medium height, the 'Indian Bean Tree', *Catalpa bignonioides,* branches strongly and has stout twigs and enormous leaves and so appears very large in scale. Similarly, where a large scale is necessary, it

The use of climbers such as Clematis montana rubens ***(below)*** *will soften the hard lines of the house.*

may be modified by using a big tree with fine tracery and small leaves.

Linking the Garden and House

The house and garden can be closely linked by extending perpendicular .lines from points around the house, such as from the corners of walls and the edges of doors and windows. Planting around the foundations of the house and using climbers trained up the walls will help to reduce the sudden junction of vertical and horizontal planes. By softening the hard architectural lines, the house will merge more easily into the garden environment.

Water

The tranquility of water always makes a commanding feature and, when used properly, brings the garden life and poetry. Still water will give beautiful reflections, adding an extra dimension to the garden and making a busy space look larger and more relaxed. Care must be taken in providing the correct conditions to prevent stagnation, however, so as to avoid the dead plants and undesirable insects that will result. Moving water, fountains or waterfalls,

***Above.** By working outwards from the lines and angles of a house, the building and garden can be successfully combined. The colours of weathered railway sleepers and terracotta tiles tone well with the house bricks.*

__Opposite page.__ A simple fountain playing over a rock and shallow pool brings this small Japanese garden to life.

has a slightly different attraction, filling the garden with sound and movement.

The dominating effect of water makes its scale and positioning of utmost importance. It can be sited either as a focal point or as a surprise element, but it should not be placed where it will detract from a view or another feature of the garden.

As water will fill any given shape it lends itself to both formal and informal gardens, and works particularly well with other landscaping features such as sculpture, lighting or natural stone in the form of cobble beaches or in a 'natural' rock garden. So its uses can be very varied, of a style to suit almost every taste.

Water can be a real liability when children are in the garden, however. But careful consideration of the design can avoid danger. A raised pool, for example, will help keep children out of the water, and by supporting a sturdy metal grid on bricks just below the surface of the water or part-filling the pool with broken stone or cobbles, the depth of the water can be reduced. These solutions retain the aesthetic appeal that fencing or netting over the pool certainly would not.

One final important point to note is the colour of the pool lining. Black is most often recommended, as it provides a good background, lending the pool depth, and interferes far less with reflections than the blue or beige of cheaper liners or the grey of concrete.

This narrow watercourse and rock garden (__below__) has been excellently constructed to mimic a natural stream.

CHAPTER
CONSIDERATIONS
THREE

MAKING A SURVEY

BEFORE SETTING ABOUT the creation of your new garden, you will want to examine closely what you have already got: its shape and size, and any existing features that are to be retained. It is worth taking care at this stage, as mistakes in initial measuring may mean alterations to the new plan when it is laid out on site.

For a completely rectangular plot, this survey will consist of measuring around the boundaries and house, utilizing these as base lines from which other points are fixed using offsets. In reality, very few gardens are so regular, and although the baseline/offset method can be used in part, a system of triangulation might be better for fixing many points. When using triangulation it is assumed that the walls of the house are straight and square (unless the house is particularly ancient). Once these have been measured, two points may be established as the main points of the triangle (see diagrams). With a complicated layout, further points can be fixed to be used as secondary triangulation points, but this could lead to errors and should be kept to a minimum. Wherever possible, measurements should be checked to ensure accuracy.

Before taking any measurements, however, a rough sketch of the plot should be drawn up to show all the features to be pinpointed: positions of slopes, services (particularly inspection covers), views to be framed, surroundings to be screened and features to be retained. This will help to prevent anything being overlooked and by marking all the measurements to be taken at the outset, the finished garden is likely to be far more successful.

Other points to note at the time of survey include height and spread of trees and shrubs; height of walls and fences; changes in level and degree of slope; soil type and drainage; places where water enters and leaves the site; materials already in use; and north points. Notes on existing microclimates will also prove useful when choosing plants or the sitting area.

ASSESSING THE POTENTIAL

Such a detailed study of the garden is likely to reveal one or two features or plants that can be used to tremendous effect. Similarly, several others will probably stand out as eyesores to be removed or shut away from sight. The vast majority, however, will fall somewhere between the two, and will have to be assessed on their individual merits. A points system can be used to compare various features on their relative worth, and in such a scheme, points would be awarded for such things as aesthetic value, suitability to site, practicality and projected life span.

Existing features, particularly trees and

A simple plot may be measured around the house and boundaries, using offsets to fix other features. A diagonal measurement can be used to check whether or not the area is rectangular.

More complex sites may be more accurately surveyed by using a system of triangulation.

N.B. Arrows denote measurements to be taken.

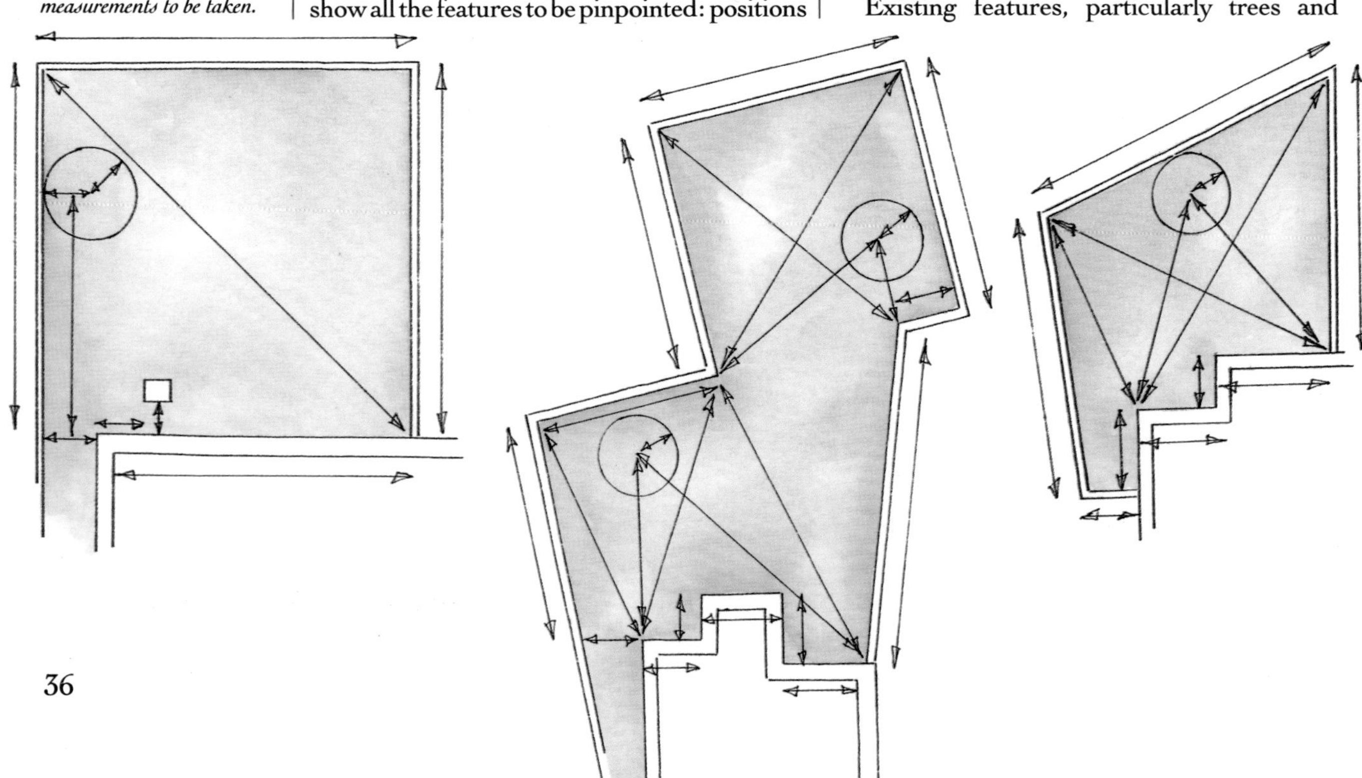

Left. A solid, traditional feel has been created by the use of mellow terracotta tiles and clipped bays (Laurus nobilis) and suits the courtyard setting.

Below. An economical design should work just as well as its more expensive counterpart. A boldly informal path of concrete paving slabs cuts through the gravel past an interesting collection of pots and plants.

*A quiet secluded corner for sitting and eating may be all that is required from the garden (**right**).*

established shrubs, will give a sense of maturity to the garden, providing scale and possibly screening. Where they can, such features should be retained, worked into the design in such a way that they provide a framework for new planting. Short-lived or diseased plants contribute little, and these, as well as plants that create an imbalance in the garden should be discarded at an early stage.

Deciding to retain or remove hard landscaping features, such as walls, can be difficult and replacement will doubtless be expensive. Funds could perhaps be put to better use elsewhere in the garden. All existing materials — including the condition of paving and walls should be examined carefully, and nothing should be discarded lightly.

Occasionally, a seemingly worthless item can be given a new lease of life by using it in a different way. An old tree stump could be incorporated as a sculptural element, for example, covered with a variety of climbing plants; or hollowed out and used as a tub in which to grow mint, for example.

SUITABILITY FOR USE

If a garden is to be of any real use, it must be related to what is required from the limited space available. If it is intended to be used mainly by children, flat hard surfacing and various play features may be of prime importance. On the other hand, a plantsman's garden will have very different characteristics, perhaps including raised beds, a scree area and bog-and-water garden.

Establishing garden use is quickly done by listing all the family's requirements, including items such as rubbish bin stores or a washing line. As space is often restricted, a strict order of priority should be fixed. Remember that the needs of the family will change over a number of years: a garden entirely devoted to young children is likely to become largely redundant in a few short years, and stand in need of considerable restructuring. If possible, it is better to include features of dual use or those that can easily be converted. A brick sandpit, for instance, could be turned into a raised bed or even a small formal pool. With careful planting, a whole new effect could be produced.

If the garden is to be used by the same family for many years, perhaps the end use should be the one planned for in the layout, employing short term measures to adapt some features to make it suitable for children.

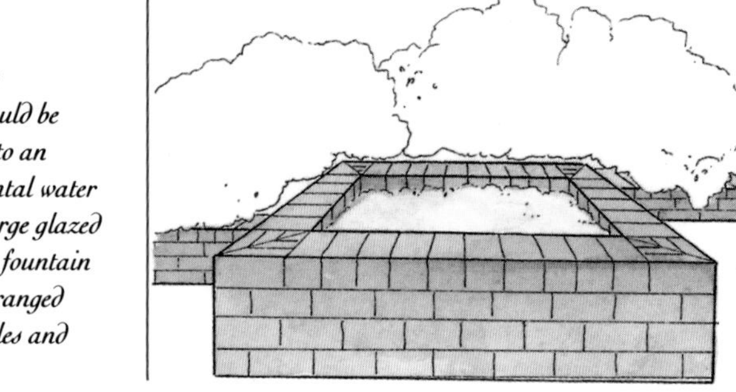

***Right.** A simple raised sandpit could be easily converted to an attractive incidental water feature with a large glazed jug adapted as a fountain and carefully arranged water-worn cobbles and irises.*

Cost

The overriding factor in the creation of any garden is the cost of construction, but the continuing cost of upkeep or maintenance is also important. To keep maintenance requirements to an acceptable level, care should be taken at the design stage. Whatever the investment, however, a garden should still work well. The same basic framework should be used for any price range.

Fences may be installed in place of walls, and grass and gravel can be substituted for paving. Such 'soft' treatments have the benefit of being more easily replaced with their 'harder' alternatives should money become available, although it is worth noting that the softer options normally require more maintenance. Aids to upkeep — such as paved mowing strips and bark mulches to border areas — can add considerably to the initial cost. Investment in initial construction is worthwhile in the long run.

A small sand pit is set in an area of hard paving ***(below)*** *goes a long way to satisfy a child's need for active play and can fit neatly into the overall scheme.*

STYLE

Gardens should be individual, each with its own identity governed by its immediate environment. Its particular style will have been laid down by the owner to suit his or her personal need. Of the many identifiable styles, a few of the most prominent are outlined below and can be used singly or in combination, depending on the space available and effect desired:

The Outdoor Room. Here the garden is treated purely as an extension to the house, with great emphasis being placed on shelter and privacy. Tall and vigorous planting is often employed to emphasize the feeling of seclusion and tranquillity. Since this type of garden is used frequently, a large area of hard surfacing is probably necessary to withstand heavy wear. Certain 'living requirements' such as seating, barbecues, water features and lighting all make the area more usable. A pergola — which can be covered — will allow the area to be used for more of the year.

The Family Garden. For a family garden, a reasonably sized terrace should be considered essential as it provides an area for children to

***Above.** The two sketches illustrate different themes based on the same design. The use of hard materials **(top)** gives a low-maintenance garden but one which may be expensive to build. The alternative **(below)** substitutes lawn for the upper paved area, uses railway sleepers to form the raised bed and rocks to replace the low retaining wall. So the garden performs the same basic functions for a lower outlay.*

play. Garden boundaries must be impenetrable, and with young children the whole area should be clearly visible from the house; older children may enjoy more secluded areas and a hideout to play in. A paved path makes a good cycle track and keeps bicycles off the plants, and where space permits, special play furniture — sand pits, paddling pools, rope swings, a small built-in adventure area or even a bare wall for ball games — keeps children amused. Such structures can all be extended, altered or removed as the children mature.

As with all designs, planting will put life into the garden. Border areas should be well stocked but avoid plants with poisonous leaves, berries and seeds at all costs. From a young age, children can be educated to appreciate the beauties of the garden and may benefit from having their own small plot to experiment with.

Above. *The Foxglove* (Digitalis purpurea) *is a handsome yet tough herbaceous plant which re-seeds itself readily in good conditions and so can withstand occasional mistreatment by children and animals.*

If the garden is to be used by an active family, space must be set aside for games and recreation ***(left)****.*

The plantsman's garden. For many keen amateur gardners, and in many cases the professional too, plants are the most important element in a garden. Most people wish to display as wide a collection of plant species as possible but it is important that they are all shown to their full advantage. This is helped by a strong sense of design — making good use of the design basics as discussed in Chapter 2 — and the inclusion of interesting features.

Although it may not be desirable to have bold groups of plants, careful arrangement of specimens in areas of like kind or similar geographical distribution will achieve a reasonable degree of continuity.

The wildlife garden. As awareness of the importance of conservation grows, the wildlife garden is increasingly seen as a way of personally contributing to the preservation of the environment. The degree to which the garden is given over to nature depends largely on personal taste and the functions it has to perform. A number of very simple steps will help encourage wildlife into the area. To bring insects, animals and birds into the garden the most obvious step is to provide food. While well-stocked bird tables are becoming increasingly important to birdlife during the winter, natural feeding is to be favoured.

A collection of conifers ***(above)*** *with a wide variety of shape, colour and form which may appeal to the plantsman while retaining a sense of unity.*

Inclusion of nectar-rich flowers, especially wild flowers, will help to bring butterflies into the garden. They are also particularly attracted to species of *Buddleia* and *Sedum*, specimens of which are rarely without one or two such visitors during the summer months. By avoiding the use of any pesticides at all, insect-eating birds are presented with an abundance of unpoisoned food. Other birds will benefit from a range of berry and seed-producing shrubs and trees, and it is worth noting that the brighter red and orange berries are more readily eaten than paler colours.

Suitable habitats have to be formed for both the animal life and the plant life that supports it. A meadow area with wild flowers and naturalized bulbs is not easy to set up, but it will provide an area of considerable beauty. Allowing some garden litter to remain, such as a stack of logs which stand and rot, or creating bog area, provides a natural, rich environment which will be favoured by insects, small animals and birds.

Wherever possible, the use of natural materials helps to create a feel of the wild. Heavy timber is ideal for retaining walls and for informal steps, although harder treatments might be better near the house.

The cottage garden. Originating in Victorian times, this type of garden was created by rural cottagers who sought to grow everything they needed. Plants were included not only for their

Ornamental cabbage provides an element of fun to a foliage bedding scheme ***(left)***

The use of natural materials sets the scene in the wildlife garden ***(right)*** *Careful management of grass areas allows wild flowers to set seed and flourish.*

floral display but also for medicinal properties. There would also be food crops, herbs, dye plants and those used to perfume the house, all seemingly thrown together in tightly packed beds. The ordered chaos that resulted was a riot of colour and provides much inspiration and delight to today's gardeners. Although nowadays, not many people have the rural setting naturally associated with the cottage garden, the same ideas can be scaled down and incorporated into smaller plots adapting them for personal need.

Landscaping materials should be chosen principally to complement the plants, selecting only the most mellow colours. Garden ornaments should be kept to a minimum, with simple designs, which leaves the tumbling mass of plants and flowers to create the atmosphere and display. Features such as picket fences, dry stone walls and gravel paths would all be in their element in this situation.

Cushion-and mat-forming plants, particularly those with scented foliage, can be planted between the paving, where they will release a powerful aroma if they are stepped on. Taller species such as *Verbascum, Alchemilla* and *Sisyrinchium* will all readily seed themselves if allowed, helping to blur the garden colouring into a wonderfully natural concoction.

House walls, fences and trellises should all be used as supports for a wide variety of climbers, wall shrubs, runner beans or sweet peas. Summer jasmine and climbing roses grown around the house give off a delicious sweet scent in the summer.

The cottage garden is normally considered to require little maintenance. But a truly traditional effect will probably require staking the taller herbaceous plants for support, and periodic splitting and replanting will be necessary to retain the health of most herbaceous species. In general, though, such maintenance would be of a more sporadic nature than in a more ordered garden.

Above. Aubrietia *and* Arabis *though often used are always effective trailing over low retaining walls or creeping over the edges of paving.*

Opposite page. *The unrestrained, almost unkempt, nature of the planting gives a cottage garden appeal to this paved terrace which is based on a circular theme.*

Raked gravel and slabs of natural stone are two of the basic ingredients in a Japanese-style garden ***(right)****.*

The Japanese garden. One thing above all others that links the gardens of Japan is their size. The chronic lack of space that exists has led to the creation of particularly small gardens, usually requiring high walls for privacy.

The Japanese have a centuries-old, religiously orientated tradition of design, and compensate for the small size of gardens by exploiting the beauty and significance of every resource. The uncomplicated layout relies on the contrasting of simple shapes against one another and is used to represent the awesomeness of the natural landscape which the Japanese revere.

The spirit of Japanese design can be found in many western gardens and has induced an appreciation of texture and shape in stone, water and plants – the principal elements of a Japanese garden. It is a style that is well suited to small gardens, particularly those which want to take on a more pictorial quality, to be viewed from the house or terrace. The juxtaposition of

***Left.** This tiny courtyard is packed with interest. Natural stone, stone artefacts and foliage plants such as the Japanese maple* (Acer palmatum) *and* Mahonia japonica *contribute equally to its appeal.*

***Left.** A sea of fine gravel gives way to a landscape of rocks and carefully manicured plants. Simplicity is the keynote.*

***Right.** The bright green stems of* Cornus stolonifera *'Flaviramea' add an extra element of display to the garden in winter.*

various elements will not necessarily have the same religious connotations in the western garden, but should still be undertaken with careful consideration.

One or more Japanese features can be incorporated into the design in the shape of stone ornaments, bamboo screens, stepping stones across gravel and water, and so on. Plants should be selected for interesting form and varying leaf texture, using colour sparingly but in bold splashes.

EFFICIENT USE OF SPACE

Anyone who has gardened in a small space for any length of time will know that limited areas must be exploited to the full. Throughout the various stages of design, avoid wasting space and creating awkward corners. It is important to form a good ground pattern, as discussed earlier, by projecting lines from the house and other strong points around the garden, which provide a focus for planting. By juggling the various elements needed in the garden the most economical, workable and aesthetic arrangement can be found.

Features that perform more than one task save space and increase the garden's usefulness: steps between levels and retaining walls are excellent examples of this, as they also make good, informal seating if constructed to the correct dimensions.

Careful attention to planting can also pay dividends. A plant with two, or more, special characteristics — foliage, fruit, autumn colour, bark, etc — will give a far more concentrated display than a plant with only one. A large shrub or tree could have its limited period of display improved by training an attractive climber up into its branches, but the climber should complement the host and should not be positioned too close to its base, as it will compete for water and nutrients.

A mass of creamy white flowers of Pyracantha *are produced in summer* ***(left)*** *and are followed in the autumn by brightly coloured bunches of berries* ***(opposite page)*** *which show well against the backcloth of dark evergreen leaves and are attractive to birds.*

Left. *Well planned lighting makes the garden an inviting place for an evening of relaxation or entertaining.*

Right. *Globe lights throw soft even lighting over their surroundings, highlighting those behind them and silhouetting those in front.*

Below. *Many different types of lamp are available and should be carefully selected to suit the site and situation: a) wall mounted; b) uplighter set in ground; c) low level downlighter; d) spotlights set on movable spikes; e) globe light, may be low level or as a standard lamp; f) brick light set in low wall.*

Lighting

Kit-form low voltage lighting sets are commonly available and easy to install, but are fairly limited in their use. A more complete set-up which lights a terrace and garden, possibly providing flood lighting to warn off intruders, would be a better investment; it should be connected directly to the mains on a separate circuit by a professional electrician using armoured cable and waterproof fittings. A new style circuit breaker is also to be recommended for outdoor electrical installations.

White light is the only colour that should be considered although various 'warm' and 'cold' tones are produced by using different bulbs. Spotlights used to shine on to shrubs should be movable so they can be used to highlight different plants as they come into effect. Uplighters will throw light high into trees to create interesting patterns with the branches. And closer to the ground, paths, drives and particularly steps should be lit with wide-beamed, or 'brick' lights set into adjacent walls.

Above. *The front garden should reflect your own personality. A passion for gardening is clearly exhibited in this suburban garden teeming with annuals, roses and dahlias.*

For paved patios a dual lighting system could be used with both dimmer lights and brighter floodlighting. Whatever lighting is installed, great care must be taken to shield the light source from direct view, as glare can easily be a problem, spoiling the desired effect.

FRONT GARDENS

Although the same basic design principles should be used on front and back gardens alike, the front garden is your display on the outside world and, as such, should reflect your own personality and ideas. The focus of the front garden is the house entrance. Access should be straightforward with suitably wide paths and level, hard-wearing surfaces. Steps should be easily negotiable with handrails provided for flights of more than three or four steps. Careful planting can guide visitors and emphasize the correct entrance. Lines of details running through paved areas, perhaps in the form of brick edging, pots, tubs and steps can all accentuate the entrance if correctly placed.

The law rarely affects the garden designer, but the three major areas of concern are: planning permission, building regulations and Tree Preservation Orders (TPOs).

Building regulations are required to ensure than construction work is carried out to a safe standard, but normally only applied to major constructional work concerning the house or other buildings.

Planning permission is needed for any major building work, particularly for structures in front of a house or for a wall fronting onto a public highway. New or altered entrances and boundary walls may well require planning permission, but an application is unlikely to succeed if the access is near a bend or junction of a major road, or if the wall interferes with drivers' sight lines in some way.

Tree Preservation Orders are usually only placed on trees that are important to the general landscape, particularly large forest-type trees. It is often desirable to retain such a major feature in the garden for the shelter it provides, but the casting of heavy shade and associated problems may make it lose favour in the gardener's eyes. In such a case the local authority can be approached, but their advice and guidelines must be obeyed.

Left. *The repetition of colour and an easily negotiable path lead the visitor to the partially obscured door.*

CHAPTER
FEATURES
FOUR

__This page.__ Paving may be laid in many different styles. A few are shown here: a) large slabs of natural stone traditionally laid around small 'key' stones; b) another traditional style of laying various-sized slabs of stone in even bands or 'tramlines'; c) random stone may be laid with ease around curves while rectangular slabs would require cutting; d) using two or more sizes of concrete paving slabs can result in attractive patterns; e) square paving slabs may be laid within a pattern of brick to heighten visual interest.

__Opposite page, bottom.__ The combination of concrete slabs with other paving types such as brick and gravel allows many interesting variations.

The mellow tones of natural stone (__below__) blend easily with the colours of the garden. The laying pattern is a traditional 'tram-line' style.

Paving

THE WEALTH of paving materials available from gardening and DIY centres can make their selection difficult. However, choosing on a basis of cost and any existing materials may help, and the breakdown of materials below should also prove a useful starting point.

Natural stone. This tends to be expensive and also involves considerable transportation costs. In an area where the natural rock is suitable for paving, however, use of stone may well be more suitable than other paving types.

Paving stone comes in different shapes, which include random pieces — irregular shapes and thicknesses; dressed pieces — rectangular shapes; or sawn pieces — rectangular with smooth surfaces. A variety of colours and shades is available, depending on the type of stone selected.

Dressed stone is easiest to lay successfully and is more polished in appearance than random stone, but using random stone in areas where curves feature strongly saves a good deal of cutting. It lends itself well to less formal situations. Sawn stone tends to be too finished for garden paving, and is, perhaps, better suited to interior use.

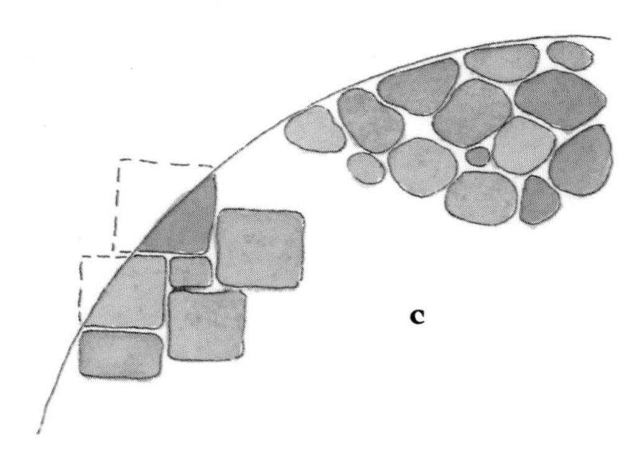

Where available, reclaimed, second-hand stone has the advantage of being weathered and therefore lends character and age to a newly-paved garden.

Concrete. Either laid as required or used as pre-formed slabs, concrete plays a great part in many gardens. The multitude of finishes that can now be obtained makes it increasingly useful. Similar sized paving slabs can form a regular pattern, or a number of different sizes combined give a more complex arrangement. A

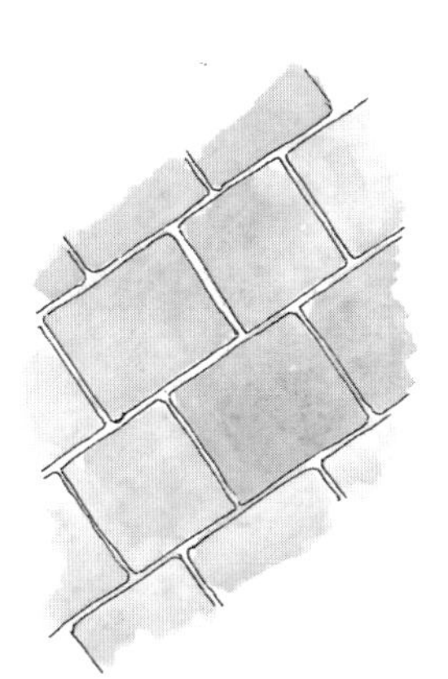

Left. A simple mixture of square end and rectangular paving slabs can easily mimic more traditional styles.

Right. Tiny carpeting plants thrive in niches between the paving and increase the variations in texture in the brick and stone.

good effect can be produced by laying slabs within 'tramlines': various sizes of slabs are used but laid within set lines running along or across the garden. This increases the apparent visual length or width of the garden.

Above. *45° herringbone (bricks laid flat at 45° to edging).*

Above. *90° herringbone (bricks laid flat at 90° to edging).*

Above. *Basketweave (bricks laid flat).*

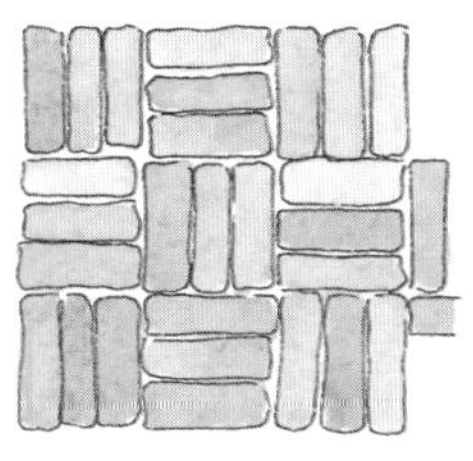

Above. *Basketweave (bricks laid on edge).*

Above. *Running basketweave (bonding gives greater sense of direction).*

'In situ' concrete is more commonly used for utility areas. The aggregate can be exposed, or it can be given a brushed finish for texture. The appearance of squares or rectangles of concrete is much improved by bordering them with bricks or other small unit paving; these can be used to create a strong ground pattern where this is desired.

Brick. Brick is a very pleasing medium to work with in the garden, as its small size makes it suitable for irregular shapes and angles, and its usually warm colour can be used to contrast and complement other paving and building materials. If selected to match the house, the bricks will have a unifying effect, visually tying the house and the garden together.

Bricks that are to be used as paving should be selected for their ability to withstand frost if your area is prone to frost; soft bricks will soon have their face shattered by the repeated action of freezing and thawing, leaving an uneven, unattractive and possibly unsafe surface. Re-

*Large rounds of timber cut from the trunk of a tree provide a pleasantly informal stepping-stone path **(right)** that is totally in keeping with the wooded setting.*

cently the production of special clay paving blocks which do not shatter has boomed, and there is now a complete range of colours with complementary kerbing blocks and matching walling bricks available. These clay paviors have the additional benefit of greater strength than ordinary bricks, and may be used as a flexible paving (that is laid without a rigid base) for both driveways and patios.

Small unit paving. This includes bricks and the smallest of the pre-cast concrete pavings, but also takes in items such as granite setts and cobbles which are increasing in popularity. Their diminitive size makes them extremely suitable for the small garden, and allows them to be laid in radial as well as rectilinear patterns.

Used on their own, setts and cobbles give an interesting but uniform surface which acts as a good foil for planting, etc. Alternatively, they may be mixed or contrasted with larger paving types to create bold patterns.

Timber. Although timber can be successfully used as a paving when the area is only used occasionally, its main drawback is its slippery

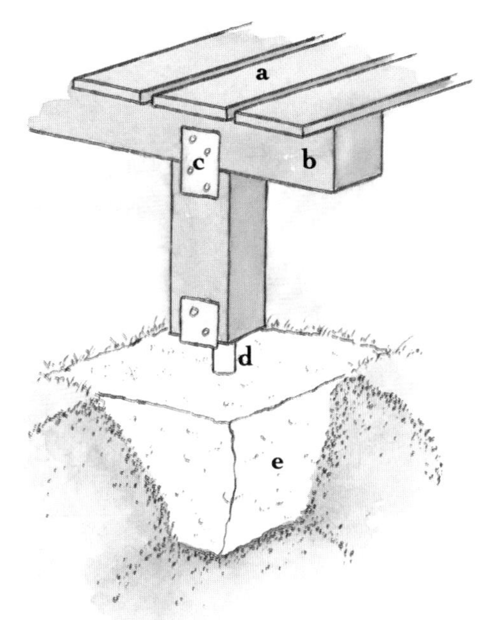

Far left. *Small concrete blocks are a tough, hard-wearing paving which can mellow considerably. Their scale can be of considerable use in the smaller garden.*

Left. *Timber decking should be supported clear of the ground by strong joists and with sufficient air gaps to allow rapid drying. Timber posts should be set clear off the ground by a metal bracket set in a substantial concrete footing.*

Key: a) timber decking with air gaps; b) joists; c) metal tie; d) post supported clear of the ground; e) concrete foundation.

Left. *Squares of timber decking set as stepping stones over gravel. The ridged timber surface will give good grip even when it is wet.*

nature when wet. This increases as a layer of algae and moss slowly builds up on the surface, so it is not sensible to use wood for main paths and thoroughfares.

By its very nature, timber is in keeping with woodland situations and can be used to help re-create similar effects in the garden. Heavy timbers such as railway sleepers make useful steps, or they can be set in the ground as stepping stones or continuous paving. Rounds cut from tree trunks can be set on sand to provide an effective surface. The gaps should be filled in with smaller rounds, gravel, or wood and bark chippings to make the area easier to use.

Wood and bark chippings are now commonly used as a planting mulch, but are also useful as loose surfacing on paths, edged by cordwood or edging board pegged in position.

Timber decking can produce a clean, striking surface. Supported above the ground on joists, the timber dries quickly to leave a dry and safe surface. Such treatment is suited to leisure areas around swimming pools, etc, where the drainage/air gaps are unlikely to be a problem and where a softer, more flexible surface might be preferred over stone or concrete.

Gravel. Gravel and stone chippings are often seen simply as a cheaper alternative to other paving surfaces, while, in fact, they can be admirable materials in their own right. Retained with an edging of brick, stone or timber, they can fit into any shape (which is very useful for small areas) and provide a good backing for foliage or tubs. Plants can be selectively planted through the gravel to give a more informal feel in desired areas.

It must be remembered that each of the different paving types requires a foundation or base. These will vary widely depending on the situation of the garden and relative use the

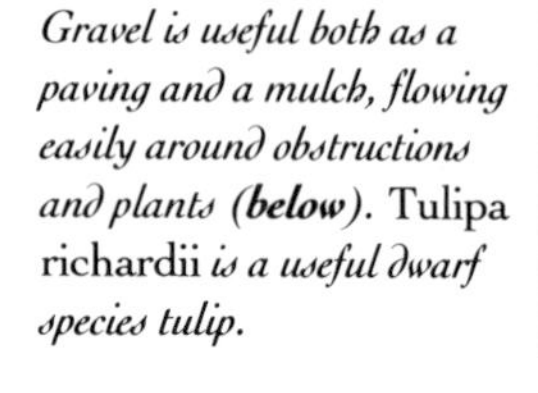

*Gravel is useful both as a paving and a mulch, flowing easily around obstructions and plants (**below**).* Tulipa richardii *is a useful dwarf species tulip.*

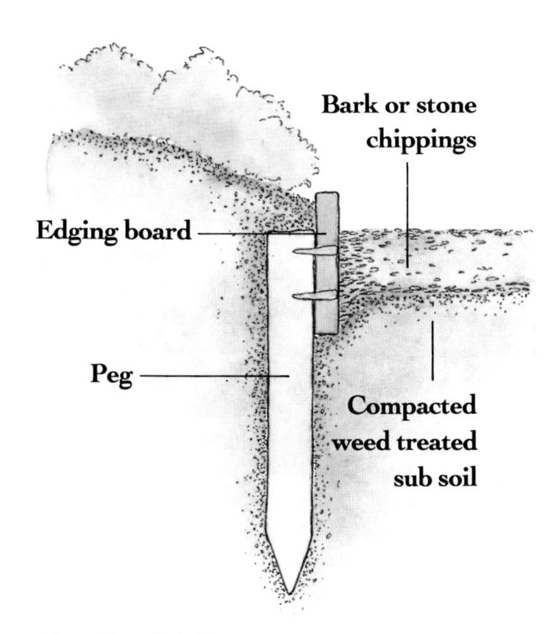

Above. *Treated timber boards provide a suitable edging for areas of gravel, or timber or bark chippings.*

Secure fixing to a stout timber peg provides stability.

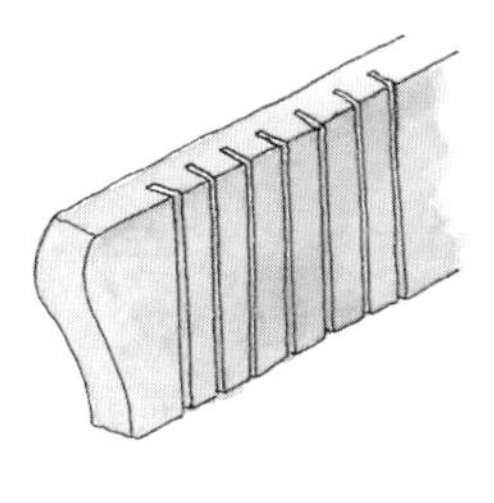

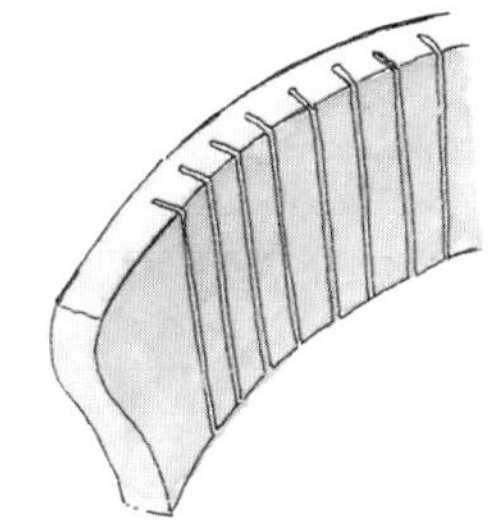

Above. *Make a series of vertical saw cuts part-way through the board to bend it around quite a tight radius.*

area is likely to receive. However, careful inspection of the photographs and illustrations in the book, which show a wide variety of paving types, will help to establish the various situations in which they could be best used. Advice on laying the appropriate foundations can be obtained from suppliers or manufacturers, whose brochures often include instructions for use and installation.

Walls

Constructed from natural stone, concrete or bricks, walls make the strongest and most imposing boundaries and divisions with the garden. As they are permanent in nature, they will in time lend the garden a sense of continuity and coherence.

The inherent beauty of natural stone is exhibited clearly in this dry stone wall ***(above)****. The cushion-forming* Sempervivium *amongst other plants, has been grown in a tiny niche to provide further appeal.*

Natural stone. As with paving, natural stone is found in a random or dressed state, depending on the finish required. Random stone may be used on its own, or 'dry' (unbonded), or with mortar to bond the pieces together. Dry stone walls are very attractive but difficult to construct properly or with any degree of stability, and require a lot of work and skill. Building the wall with a suitable batter on each side makes a safer structure and is easier to construct — as long as you have the patience.

Dry stone walling is particularly suitable for low retaining walls, and if soil is compacted into the gaps, small alpine plants can be rooted through. Stability is provided by a wide concrete or stone foundation, by building the wall to a batter, and by inserting occasional long stones to tie the wall back into the mass of soil.

Walls built with mortar are much easier to construct, although the mortar can detract from the appearance of the stone. Stones of different sizes will give a random wall, or the stones can be sorted into roughly equal

Right. *A dry stone retaining wall should be built to a backwood leaning batter with occasional long stones to tie back into the body of soil. A simple stone mowing edge will make the area much easier to mow. Key: a) plants growing through wall (positioned during construction); b) concrete foundation; c) stone mowing edge; d) lawn.*

thicknesses and laid in level courses. Dressed stone is laid in even layers to produce a coursed wall, although 'jump' blocks several courses high may be incorporated.

Both types of wall will require a coping, which usually consists of large flat stones and serves to waterproof the wall.

Bricks and blocks. Concrete or reconstituted stone blocks are more commonly available than those of natural stone. All walls of these materials should be based on a firm concrete foundation and built in a suitable bonding pattern (as illustrated) so that the vertical joints do not coincide. Where a particular decorative pattern where the bonds do coincide is desired, strips of reinforcing mesh should be set into and along the horizontal mortar bed at regular intervals to aid stability.

Concrete blocks tend to be plain to look at, but can be rendered to provide a good surface for painting, or used as a strong backing to which a facing of brick or natural stone can be fixed with mortar and metal ties. The latter is a practical construction for retaining walls, where only one face is visible.

Reconstituted stone is, by and large, a poor alternative to natural stone. But it can be used to reasonable effect where cream and beige tones are required to match paving stones, or as a contrast to dark foliage and timber.

Below. *Bricks of varying colours may be used to highlight the bonding pattern. Here red and grey bricks are laid in Flemish bond.*

Left. *A 'half brick' wall (4"/10.25cm wide) built in stretcher bond, showing how a pier should be bonded in.*

Below left. *A 8½"/21.5cm wide, or single brick wall constructed in Flemish bond with alternate headers (small face) and stretchers (long face) in each course.*

The combination of brickwork with stone copings, pier caps and finials can make for a particularly fine wall ***(far left)***

Brick is perhaps the most flexible of building materials. It works well for either very plain and simple walls, which are a backcloth to the garden, or for more detailed work, as a feature in its own right, which may use specially-shaped bullnose, plinth or cant bricks. Such bricks, however, are expensive and should be used sparingly: railings, wrought iron work, and stone finials and copings can also all be

combined with the brickwork. Such a wall would provide an imposing entrance to a larger or period house, but should not be over-stated.

The width of all walls should be proportioned to their height, and additional strengthening piers installed as necessary. Brick walls less than a brick thick (8½in/21.5 cm) tend to look flimsy and are unsatisfactory unless

__Right.__ A single brick wall constructed in English bond with alternate courses of headers (small face) and stretchers (long face). English Garden Wall bond differs from English bond by extra courses of stretchers between the header courses (__below right__).

__Above.__ A simple coping of bricks laid on edge gives a clean, functional finish. Metal ties prevent the end brick being knocked off.

__Below.__ The addition of a double tile creasing below the brick on edge will further weatherproof the wall and add detail.

particularly small. Brickwork that is 8½ in/21.5 cm wide is generally suitable for walls up to 6 ft/1.80m high, but should be strengthened with piers for greater heights. In any case, piers will add interesting details to even the smallest of walls and should always be used to provide suitable end stops to a length of brickwork. Remember also to allow expansion joints in walls over 11 yards (approximately 10m) in length.

Retaining walls will need to be thicker than free-standing walls to withstand the force of soil bearing down on them. Their strength can be increased by digging deeper foundations, with steel strengthening bars, and by constructing the wall to a batter. Professional advice should be sought in cases where the height of the soil to be retained is over 3ft(1m).

__Right.__ Flat or ridged copings may be made from stone or precast concrete. Narrow grooves cut in the underside of the coping will ensure any water falling on the coping drips clear of the brickwork.

__Below.__ The clean, crisp lines of steps made from concrete paving slabs are softened by the trailing growth of ivy.

STEPS

Although often thought of as a nuisance, steps have enormous potential to create interest in the garden, with an endless variety of materials

and styles which can be used. While a garden with a gentle but appreciable slope provides the most suitable site for garden steps, even a flat garden has one or two possibilities.

By cutting and filling an area of garden, an apparent disparity of levels is produced and a step or two can be installed. By raising an area of paving a step will automatically be created,

Left. *Simple stone steps give an elegant transition between a path of granite setts and a paved upper terrace.*

Left. *A large, flat expanse of paving does little to excite visually* ***(above)****. Even by putting in just a small raised area interest is immediately created* ***(below)****.*

Opposite page, centre. *By offsetting stone steps and allowing the planting to encroach, a completely informal arrangement is produced.*

Opposite page, bottom. *More formal steps of railway sleepers and gravel ascend a grassy bank. The use of additional sleepers as a mowing edge adds a pleasing detail and helps maintenance.*

*The timber and gravel steps pictured (**left**) have been laid to make a graceful curve. By leaving the step ends undefined, the planting will spread to totally informalize the arrangement.*

breaking up the expanse of hard surfacing and making a smaller, more intimate area.

Steps need to be easily negotiable, and so the risers and treads must be of suitable size. Risers taller than 7in/18cm become an effort to climb, while treads narrower than 1ft/30cm are difficult to descend with ease. Where different levels mean a steep flight of steps, a handrail provides a sense of security. A riser of around 6in/15 cm combined with a 18in/45 cm tread gives a broad step of pleasing proportions and one that can be constructed easily from modern paving materials.

Steps onto a main thoroughfare should be straight and functional, but those elsewhere in the garden can be more decorative, with curves and circles. Changes in direction provide a welcome break from a long flight of steps, and a collection of pots would help to soften the hard, architectural lines of the steps.

Spectacular effects can come from combining steps with other features such as sculpture and water, thus making a point of real emphasis. Careful planting can add yet another dimension by softening, enclosing, and adding colour and life.

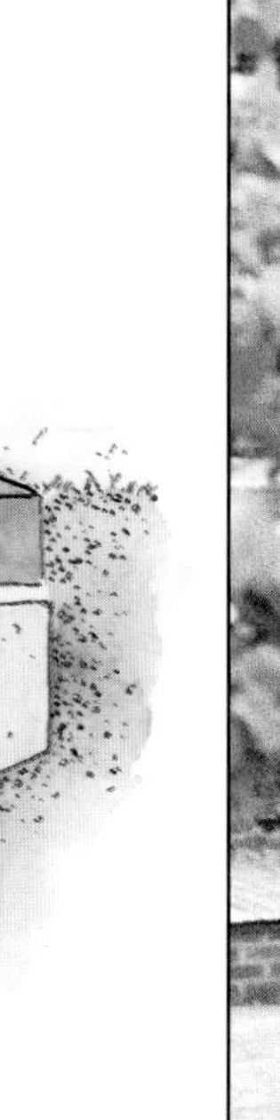

Above top. *18" x 24"/ 45 x 60cm paving slabs together with a brick-on-edge riser make an easily constructed, well proportioned set of steps.*

Above. *Steps using bricks on edge as the tread. The curved edges of bullnosed bricks make for a softer look.*

Both flights of steps will need a fairly substantial concrete footing to ensure they remain stable.

PONDS

Water, both still and moving, has enormous potential to improve a garden. The construction, shape and style of pond will all greatly influence the final atmosphere in the garden.

The effect of ice on the construction of a pool is of paramount importance if you live in a frost-prone area. During the winter months even a thin layer of ice can exert tremendous pressure on the pool sides, causing inferior

Left. *The simple movement of water brings light and life to a shady corner.*

Left. *The combination of a flight of steps and water feature can be particularly attractive.*

Left. *The sunken water garden has considerable style with the large formal pool capturing the attention.*

Next pages 70/71. *Steps, water, clipped box, statuary and brightly coloured bedding combine to make an enchanting garden.*

***Below.** Two more unusual ways of disguising butyl rubber liner involve the construction of a gently shelving cobble beach or taking the liner up behind a railway sleeper. The sleeper would be firmly fixed to other sleepers with battens or secured to pegs.*

constructions to crack and therefore to leak. Reinforced concrete in particular produces a rigid pool which requires attention and strengthening to the top section of the pool, (where the ice will form in winter), whether the pool is built above ground level or not.

Among the most suitable flexible liners is Butyl rubber, increasingly popular for its long life and easy installation. Ice presents less of a

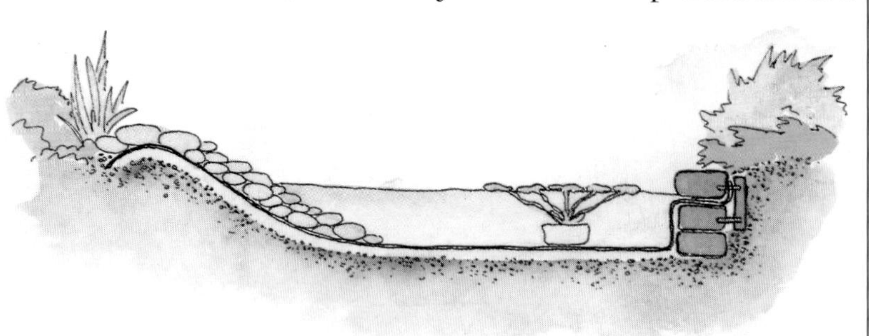

***Below.** When a rock garden is not built on a natural slope, the drop behind should be screened by larger plants. Most of the rock will remain hidden, although smaller rocks may be placed together to make them look stronger*

problem to flexible liners, although if a pool is raised it may need the added strength of reinforced concrete to help the surrounding walls withstand any sideways pressure.

Water height fluctuates with evaporation and the operation of cascades and fountains, and so the top edge of liner or concrete is often

***Right.** A raised scree bed should be constructed to give good drainage. The soil should have added grit; a surface mulch of stone chippings will help rapid surface drainage. A further drainage layer should be included below the soil.*

exposed. To overcome this, a stone or brick edge overhang will camouflage the exposed strip and water's edge with an area of deep shadow. Suitable marginal planting can achieve the same result.

The use of any water features must be governed by the overall feel of the garden. A formal layout may suggest a central pool with fountain, whereas a rock garden and cascade would be better suited to a more natural and informal layout, particularly where a change in levels is already present. Rectangular raised pools with a bubble or geyser fountain and simple fall between two levels would look more in keeping with a modern, geometric layout, as would a large, shallow reflecting pool.

Even the smallest gardens need not be without the pleasure of sound and movement that water gives. A simple wall-mounted mask fountain spurting into a stone trough takes up little space and can provide all the qualities desired. It could also be used as an incidental feature in a larger garden.

The combining of sculpture, plants and water needs careful consideration. Plants with lush foliage look luxuriant beside a pool, and upright strap-like leaves will help to balance its strong horizontal nature. Remember also the mirror-like quality of water; this should be reflected in the choice of plants placed around the pool. The sculptural element of stone can be very useful, the simple lines of water-worn rocks and cobbles providing the perfect complement to a smooth, untroubled pool.

ROCK GARDENS AND SCREES

For a rock garden to have any real effect, it must imitate an alpine scree or rock escarpment as closely as possible. Rocks should be sorted into various sizes, using the largest at the base and smaller ones higher up. Only a small proportion of the rock should be exposed, with the

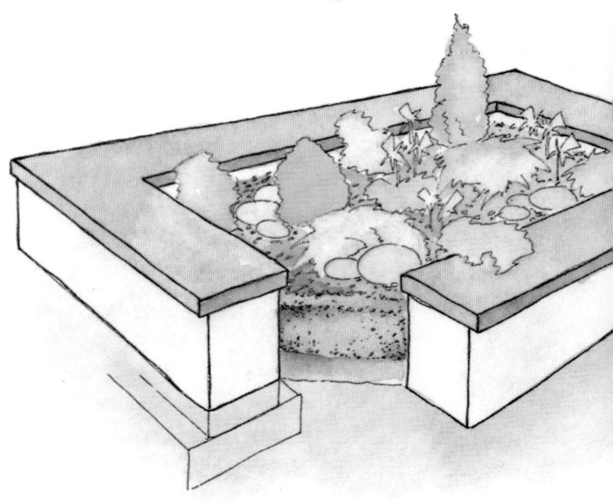

Left. *The combination of rock garden and a seemingly natural waterfall can give immense pleasure to those who can maintain such detailed planting.*

A miniature scree garden can be constructed in a large sink or pot ***(above)*** *which makes a good setting for the beauty of alpine plants.*

Right. *A framework of black-painted metal provides interesting support for a pool area and makes a good visual line with the house. The bold dark leaves of* Ligularia *provide an impressive contrast.*

remainder being buried in soil. The rock strata should be aligned in a single plane to give the effect of a natural outcrop. Smaller rocks can be carefully placed immediately next to each other to take on the appearance of a single larger piece if this effect is required.

In gardens without a natural slope, the back of the rockery may be supported by a brick or concrete block retaining wall. Such an arrangement must be heavily planted, however, and the rockery kept low to prevent it seeming out of place.

The scree garden takes its name from the bank of loose chippings found at the base of a rock face, and is easier to reproduce in a domestic garden. A small raised bed surfaced with a mulch of stone chippings and the occasional embedded rock is the ideal habitat for many alpines and dwarf conifers and shrubs. A sunny situation and suitable drainage is needed, though. A scree garden can exist simply in a large bowl or stone trough which incorporates plants and rocks of similar scale.

Trellis Work

Trellis gives immediate height to any garden design, and is the perfect support for climbing plants such as clematis or roses. It works well as a screen as it interrupts a view without completely hemming a garden in. Foliage-covered trellis is particularly useful for internal divisions in the garden, allowing occasional glimpses through to provide interest.

Traditionally constructed in squares or diamonds, trellis needs to be fairly substantial to be of any long-term use in the garden. Maintenance is difficult, if not impossible, once climbers are heavily entwined, and small timbers would quickly deteriorate thanks to rain and wind.

White-painted trellis stands out, but should not be overused as it has a tendency to make the garden seem smaller. Conversely, a dark-

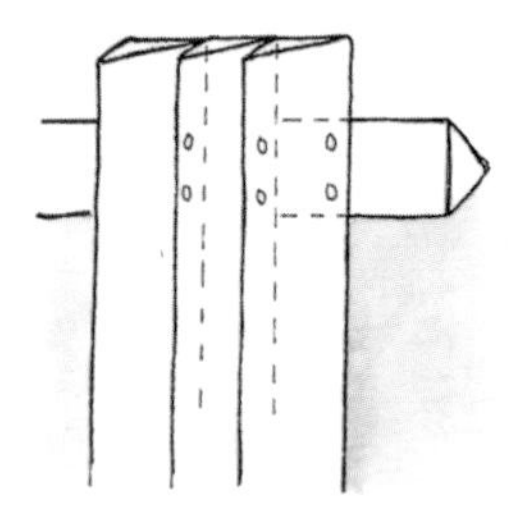

Top and above. Close boarded fence using feather edged boards, arris rails and timber gravel board.

***Above right.** Larch lap panel fence.*

***Far right.** Diagonal boards infill brick piers and a low wall.*

***Above.** Different styles of fence produced from various timber boards fixed to horizontal rails.*

stained trellis will provide a mellow, sombre framework for climbers which will merge more naturally with the surrounding planting.

Panels with curved and shaped tops can transform a plain trellis screen, and decoration of the posts with finials will create a distinctive style. Special 'perspective panels' (which can be bought ready made) can also be incorporated in a screen or against a wall to open up an apparent alley or vista, particularly when used in conjunction with a mirror.

The look of a trellised garden can be completed with a range of matching artefacts such as obelisks or spheres.

Fences

Although fences are the most obvious and cost-effective form of boundary, they need never be utilitarian or basic in appearance. The many different fencing styles available can look equally at home in a small garden or on a larger country estate.

If the boundary is to be obscured by planting, a simple but strong fence can be constructed by nailing feather-edged boards to horizontal rails which in turn have been fixed to posts set vertically in the ground. A 'gravel

board' below the fence prevents the bottom of the fence coming into contact with the ground, which would make it rot. If decay does set in, the gravel board can be removed and replaced. A simple timber capping fixed onto the top of the fence will prevent dampness from seeping into the end grain.

Ready-made fencing panels are easy to erect but generally have a shorter life span, due to the thinness of wood. Nevertheless, they are certainly worth considering as a temporary screen while new plants become established.

The picket or pallisade fence is a popular boundary, particularly for older, cottage-style properties. Posts may be painted, rounded or simply finished with finials. Round, pointed posts can be similarly finished with finials.

To create a totally unique fence, timbers can be fixed to horizontal rails between posts, or simply be fixed horizontally themselves. The variation of timber sizes and intermediate gaps allows for an endless variation of effects; by introducing bamboo into the construction for example, the fence will take on an oriental feel.

Less formal fences work best in rural situations. Although relatively short-lived, the wattle fence is attractive. Chestnut paling and wire fences are of little value on their own except to allow an open view, but used with hedges and evergreen shrubs they make an attractive screen a more effective barrier. All fencing is improved by the addition of climbers or other greenery. In the case of a chainlink fence, it can be carefully trimmed to form in effect a narrow edge.

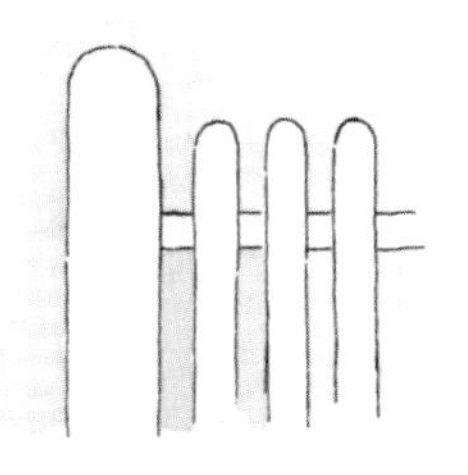

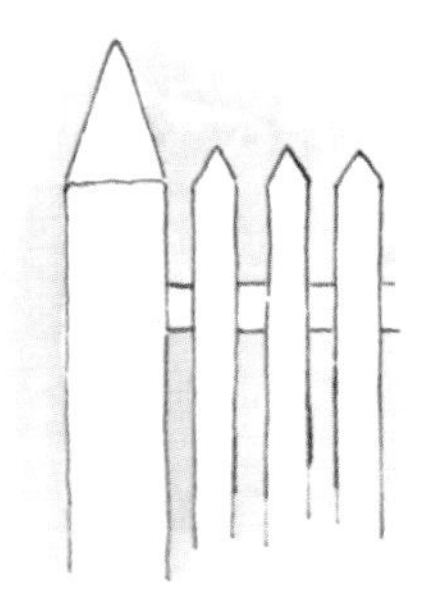

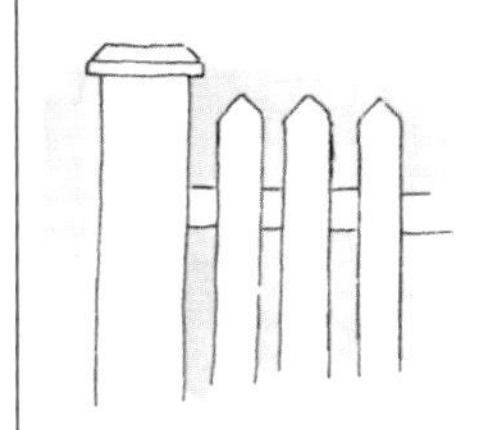

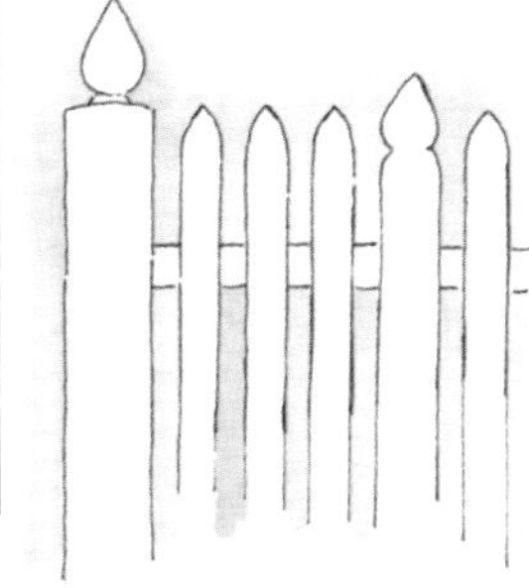

Left and right. *Various styles of picket fencing are easy to create.*

Below. *A simple timber picket fence is perfectly in keeping with the semi rural situation.*

Right. *Simple finishes for pergola beams and cross beams.*

Pergolas

In a similar way to trellis, a pergola — an arbour or garden walk arched with climbing plants — gives instant height to a garden, and in a small space utilizes the area above ground, thereby increasing the scope for plant growth.

Once the planting is established, the pergola gives a dappled shade beneath providing an enclosed and protected area. The transition from an open terrace to a path straddled and shaded by a pergola leading to an open lawn is one of the strongest, most enticing ways of guiding people out into a garden.

The pergola straddling a path can act as a frame for a suitable ornament or piece of planting. A simple seat backed by dark planting would give an ideal goal to head towards.

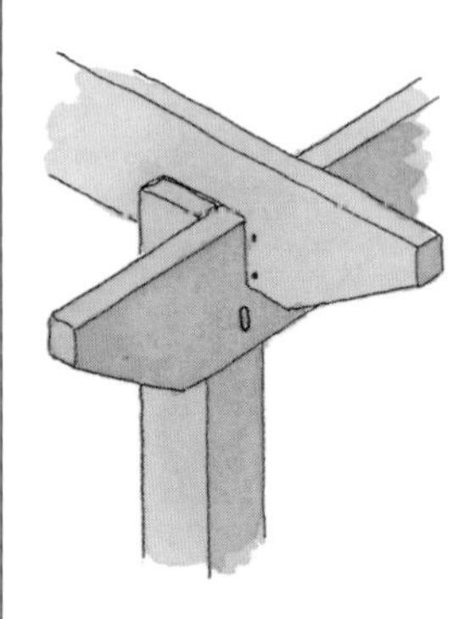

Below. *A sturdy pergola with brick piers and weathered hardwood beams and crossbeams. The generous proportions allow easy movement beneath.*

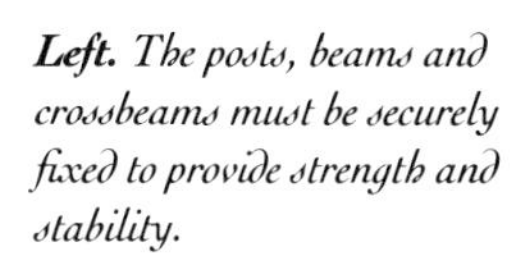

Left. *The posts, beams and crossbeams must be securely fixed to provide strength and stability.*

*A more elegant pergola **(right)** with cast iron pillars and a timber beam.*

Below. *Simply altering the direction of the cross beams can give a tremendous sense of direction.*

Pergolas also make an ideal transition from the dark of the house to the brightness of the garden. A simple covering could be used to create a loggia effect, giving protection on a cool or breezy night.

The pergola's screening properties prevent the eye straying upwards to overbearing buildings, keeping it settled down amongst the surrounding garden. If space is limited, a 'single bar' pergola constructed along the boundary or across the garden will give additional height and pleasantly enclose the garden. Its height can be adjusted to screen a line of windows or nearby telephone cables.

The construction of pergolas is generally based on timber, although steel or concrete may be used with timber posts or brick piers as support. Heavier timber is better for a solid, sturdy-looking construction and of course lasts longer. The shade and support that the pergola offers will depend on the number and frequency of crossbars installed, and the spacing between climber-bearing posts. Plastic-coated or galvanised wires stapled across the crossbars will provide additional support for climbers where necessary.

Any further finishes will obviously be selected to blend with the general style of the garden. Attendant climbers may be chosen to give a single period of massed display, or as often preferred in a small garden, as an ongoing show of flower and leaf colour.

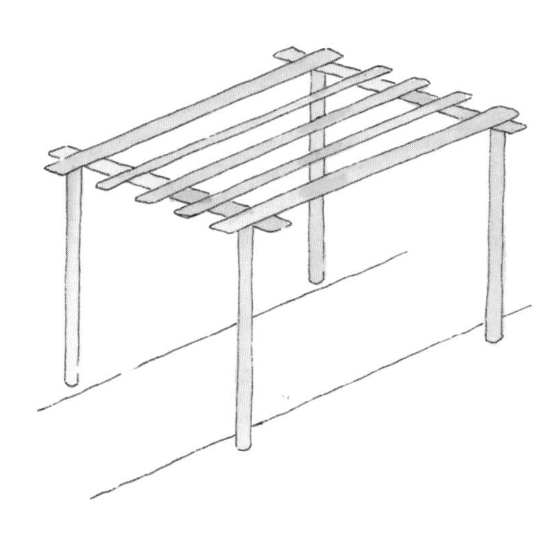

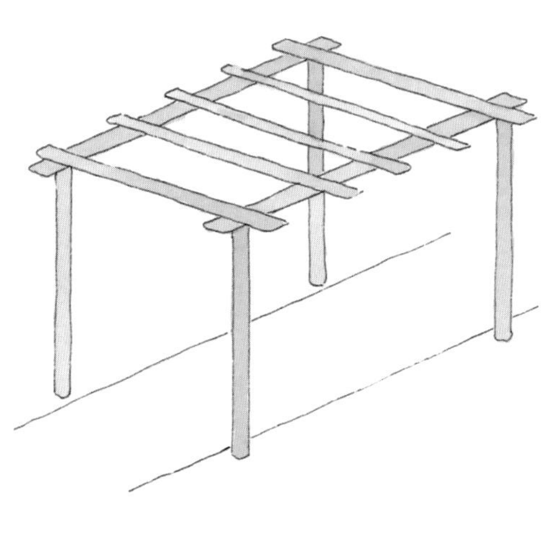

Garden ornament

Just how much ornament is included in the garden relies heavily on personal tastes, as does the choice of ornament itself. Statues, sculpture, pots and tubs will all attract the eye, and so could be used with care to create specific points of interest. Pots and tubs will help to break up and punctuate a paved terrace and are particularly useful close to the house where they can be watered frequently with ease.

Sculpture and statues combine well with water. A smaller piece used as a distant attraction needs a similarly scaled enclosure, such as a small niche. The possibilities are limited only by imagination and it is worth looking out for special additions for your garden. Simplicity of form is often the best thing to aim for.

Left. *Concrete sheep add relief and humour to a shaded lawn.*

Old chimney pots (**below**) *are harder to come by as they become more fashionable. Filled with ivy-leaved geraniums, lobelia and* Tagetes *they make a colourful display.*

CHAPTER
PLANTING
FIVE

Right. *A broad valley of white evergreen azaleas cuts between mature rhododendrons to form an impressive and colourful view.*

WHATEVER THE USE intended for a garden, plants are obviously of fundamental importance. Not only do they lend life and colour to the area, but they also provide the mass and body needed to convert a two-dimensional plan into a three-dimensional reality. Many people feel that plants and gardens are totally synonymous, each being dependent on the other.

Garden planting often suffers from a lack of thought, which wastes both time and money as the plants then require resiting or replacing. Even minor mistakes will become increasingly obvious as the planting matures and are, of course, harder to correct with time.

Before starting to plant the garden, set out to learn about the plants you would like to use – their ultimate size, growth rate, habit, leaf size and colour, flowering characteristics, and perhaps most importantly, the conditions they require for good growth.

As a starting point, the main plant groups are outlined below and the section on planting sequence will help to show how a sucessful planting plan can be built up.

PLANT GROUPS

Each of the main plant types has particular features which relate chiefly to that individual group. In many cases, such characteristics will be strong enough to influence or even dictate the group's use in the garden.

In the temperate regions of the world, deciduous trees provide the main accent points in a garden – areas of stress an emphasis – and, as such, should be used sparingly and with considerable thought.

Although the size of a tree has obvious implications on scale within the garden and may be important for screening purposes, the principle design point is the branching pattern. Trees with ascending branches lead the eye upward, while those with branches descending have the opposite effect. Such branching patterns may be utilized in directing the eye to more distant views or in holding it within the plot.

The relative strength of a tree also has a tremendous bearing on its use. Those with bold leaves and stout twigs – such as *Catalpa bignonioides* or *Rhus typhina* – and strong, sturdy looking trees typified by the oaks (*Quercus spp.*) are best planted as single specimens. Conversely, trees with fine tracery (thin branches and twigs) and smaller leaves, such as birch trees (*Betula spp.*) are more effective arranged in groups.

Those which cast dense shade, such as the horse chestnut (*Aesculus spp.*), or are hungry feeders such as ash (*Fraxinus spp.*) should be

Below. *The brightly coloured foliage of* Gleditsia triacanthos *'Sunburst' makes an outstanding focal point. Its small size and grace make it useful in even quite compact town gardens.*

avoided, particularly in smaller gardens, as they can seriously inhibit the growth of other plants near them.

Broad-leaved evergreen trees exhibit the same characteristics as their deciduous counterparts, but the dense, thick, waxy leaves obscure much of the branching pattern. This reduces their effect, particularly during the winter months when the naked framework of a deciduous tree appears as a silhouette against the sky. It is the general shape of the evergreen tree, coupled with the size, colour and posture of its leaves which are its most noticeable characteristic; only if the branches are carefully thinned out will a stronger branch pattern emerge.

Below. *The bright red, young foliage of* Pieris *'Forest Flame' provides a spectacular display in the spring. An acid soil and protection from late spring frosts are essential.*

Conifers often have a distinct outline. Their foliage, being matt, reflects little light which gives them a generally dark appearance. The long needles of pines create strong lines and texture which hold their own well against bold modern architecture. *Thuja spp.* and *Chamaecyparis spp.* are both visually softer conifers with less distinctive foliage patterns, and the various species of juniper have the tiniest needles of all. Fine needles form an almost indistinguishable

pattern which makes these the softest of all conifers in appearance, although they are probably the hardest to touch.

Many conifers are narrow and upright. This contributes to their use as accent points in a garden, and as with trees, they should be used sparingly unless they are to form part of a specific conifer garden.

Shrubs vary greatly in stature, ranging from tiny alpines to tree-like plants. In fact, the delineation between shrubs and trees is rarely clear, and in a small garden a large shrub may well produce the same effect as a tree.

Evergreen shrubs should be selected chiefly for their size, shape, texture and leaf shape as these, as with all evergreens, will be apparent all year round. Although their flowers are a welcome bonus, they rarely last more than a month or so and are of less consequence.

As with all planting, larger leaves give a coarser texture. Coarse and fine foliage should be combined with several intermediate types; remember that as the size of foliage decreases, the quantity needs to increase to retain a balanced effect.

Deciduous shrubs are 'weaker' in appearance than their evergreen counterparts, and because of this a deciduous shrub with large leaves will be required to balance an evergreen with comparatively fine foliage.

Above. *The dwarf hybrids of* Rhododendron yakushimanum *are easily fitted into a small garden. The low, white flowered* Tiarella cordifolia *provides suitable ground cover beneath.*

With deciduous shrubs, the changing seasons emphasize different characteristics. Foliage flower and bright autumn colour as the leaves prepare to fall are all worth considering, and in the case of *Cornus, Kerria,* etc, attractive coloured stems are openly displayed during the winter. Deciduous shrubs contribute to a sense of time in the garden, mourning the passing of summer as their leaves drop to the ground, and heralding the coming of spring as the new shoots burst the winter buds.

Herbaceous plants with their fleshier stems usually die down in winter, leaving the earth bare and exposed. Even weaker in appearance than deciduous shrubs, only those plants with exceptionally bold foliage are of any structural consequence; most herbaceous plants should be selected for their foliage shape and colour and, above all, their flowers.

Traditionally, herbaceous plants were set aside in distinct borders, giving a wonderful display during the summer and early autumn but being completely devoid of life in winter. Such an arrangement is not suited to a small garden, and so the blending of shrubs and herbaceous plants is now by far the most common choice. In this way, shrubs provide structure and winter display and the herbaceous plants are used to provide effective ground cover and additional flowers during the peak summer months when the garden is mainly in use. Mixing of shrubs and low

The loose feathery inflorescences of Cotinus coggygria ***(below)****. Making a larger shrub or small tree, the leaves take on brilliant tints in the autumn.*

The low mounds of grey foliage and pink or white flowers make Dianthus ***(left)*** *a valuable edging plant for a sunny spot.*

herbaceous plants has an added benefit of enabling the ground to be covered quickly as the herbaceous plants are cheaper to purchase and spread readily. When the shrubs mature, herbaceous planting is gradually displaced due to shade; this helps to avoid the competition that can also occur when shrubs are planted too close together.

Taller herbaceous plants may require staking, particularly in more exposed situations or where the plant has become drawn due to lack of light. Lower-growing species, such as *Geranium spp., Pulmonaria spp.,* and *Campanula poscharskyana,* provide masses of flowers, but they have the advantage that they need little upkeep or attention, although even these benefit from the mulching, splitting and re-planting usually associated with perennials.

Alpine plants are generally diminutive herbaceous species, and are a source of intricate beauty. Their native habitat is on the dry and open slopes of mountainous regions, and they only really give their best when similar conditions are created in the garden. Used in niches in paving or in small sink gardens or scree beds, they will slowly spread to provide bright patches of colour. The soil should be modified with grit and sharp sand to facilitate good drainage and a mulch of stone chippings will ensure a favourable cool root run.

Aquatic plants are herbaceous in nature, but specially adapted to growing in water or saturated soil. Not only are they an added attraction to a pond or water feature, but are also a fundamental part of the balanced ecosystem necessary to maintain a clear and healthy pond.

Even without this practical consideration, the beauty of their flowers and foliage would still win them a place in many gardens; a water filled half-tub is all that is required to provide a suitable habitat for these delicate plants. By using one of the dwarf hybrids, the elegance and beauty of water lillies can be introduced into a garden in this way.

Planting Sequence

The successful planting of a garden should be planned and undertaken in stages. If correctly approached, the end result will provide an attractive display and will also satisfy the fundamental issues of screening and enclosure. The various aspects of planting design may be roughly grouped into three main phases:

Structural planting. The first part of planting a garden involves the careful juxtaposition of trees and larger more solid shrubs. These will provide the main bones of the design around which the remaining planting will be draped. Around two-thirds of this structural planting should be evergreen to ensure that all the basic framework remains sound and solid throughout the winter months.

Any screening is an inherent part of the structural planting, so ensure this basic need is incorporated at the outset.

The main infill. At this second level, planting has its most functional role, filling areas to lend relief and contours to the garden. This main bulk of the planting helps to define and balance the various spaces within the layout.

Plants in this section need to be effective in their own right, but they also need to provide a suitable backdrop to the smaller ornamental plants. As with the structural planting, plants comprising the main infill should be selected for their shape and habit; again, leaf shape, texture and colour are all of similar importance. Flowering characteristics should not be totally ignored, as suitable plants with attractive flowers will add to the display.

The ornamental element. These plants are selected primarily for their decorative value. Although the leaf shape, texture and habit are still important, the decisive factor will tend to be the flowers which are characteristic of individual plants.

Bedding roses, herbaceous perennials, biennials, annuals and bulbs will all slot into this category, as will many deciduous and evergreen shrubs, depending on their size and purpose within the design. These groups are often viewed as the most interesting ingredient in the planting recipe, but their true worth will be lost if the backcloth is not properly prepared.

Planting for Effect

While all planting designs are approached in the same way, the style of planting is very much down to personal taste. Just how brightly coloured or mellow the arrangement is depends wholly on your choice of how the garden space is to be used. A more restrained planting scheme will provide a more restful air, which is often a garden's most desirable aspect, particularly to those that live and work in a town or city. A busy look can also be refreshing.

Strict colour schemes limited to particular areas will avoid untidy clashes and muddles of colour, and in consequence will give a more spectacular display.

While colour should be restrained, foliage effects can run riot. Striking foliage, such as Phormium contrasted against soft mounds of lavender or *Hebe rakaiensis* can really hold the eye; dramatic groupings can be formed by combining the strap-like leaves of Iris or *Hemerocallis spp.* with large beach cobbles or *Bergenia spp.*

Helixine with its tiny leaves or moss, creeping around the edges of paving, will emphasize individual units, and the same frame of green will also soften hard edges and draw the planting and stones together.

At the other end of the scale, trees not only provide screening and structure, but afford welcome rest from the hot sun of warm climates. In cooler areas, more open-headed varieties such as *Robinia spp.* and *Sorbus aucuparia* cast patterns of light-dappled shade across pavings and lawn.

Fragrance is often overlooked in the garden nowadays, but can contribute greatly to the overall effect; it is particularly enjoyed by those people who are blind or partially sighted. The heady scent of broom (*Cytisus spp.*) fills the senses in spring, and *Philadelphus spp.*, roses, lavender and many others are delightfully scented during the summer. In the winter months, *Chimonanthus praecox* and *Virburnum forreri* also provide scent.

Touch is a sense worth considering in a garden, with the soft silky leaves of *Stachys lanata* (lambs' ears) or the young felted stems of *Rhus typhina* (stag's horn sumach).

Wildlife will be attracted to the garden by nectar-rich flowers, autumn berries and suitable habitats. By taking all of these aspects into consideration, the garden can satisfy all the major human senses: sight, smell, touch, sound . . . and add a few herbs for taste.

Left. *A harmonious herbaceous planting of mainly blue and grey. The blue-leafed grass* Festuca glauca *makes rounded cushions in the foreground.*

Opposite page, bottom. *The herbaceous geranium species make a reliable, easily maintained display.*

Below. *Dwarf orange lilies tone beautifully with the spikey leaves of* Phormium *'Maori Sunrises' and the dark purple foliage of* Cotinus coggygria *'Royal Purple'.*

CHAPTER SIX
UP ON THE ROOF OR OUT ON A LEDGE

IN THE CRAMPED confines of the city, many people find their only outside space is a flat roof, a balcony or a window ledge. This lack of space may limit ideas, but there is no reason why what space there is should not become a green and pleasant refuge or provide an attractive outlook on the world.

Unless you are fortunate enough to live in a purpose-built block with specially structured balconies or roofs, the proposed garden will be limited by the load-bearing capacity of the building. This should be researched fully, using the services of a surveyor if necessary, to avoid later structural problems.

But whatever the load-bearing capacity, weight will be of primary importance, so examine ways of keeping it to a minimum. Plants grown in pots require less soil than those in large beds, and many plants adapt well to this as long as they are watered and fed sufficiently. Loam-free planting compost will be lighter than ordinary garden soil but as loam acts as a chemical buffer, take care that no nutrient builds up to a level where it may become toxic to the plant, by using well-balanced feeds.

Timber, plastic, fibreglass and asbestos all make excellent lightweight containers, and an unnatural appearance is soon disguised by trailing plants. Timber decking and asbestos tiles make attractive flooring, as do quarry tiles; the warm hues and small size of quarry tiles work well for a restricted roof garden and act as the perfect foil to evergreen plants.

Drainage systems must be organized before any flooring is laid, both to remove rainwater and also the large quantity of irrigation water required to keep pots and tubs moist. What

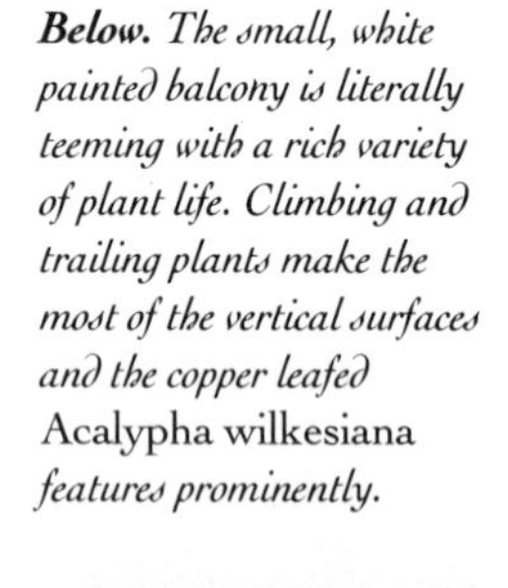

***Below.** The small, white painted balcony is literally teeming with a rich variety of plant life. Climbing and trailing plants make the most of the vertical surfaces and the copper leafed* Acalypha wilkesiana *features prominently.*

must be avoided at all costs is seepage of water into the building structure. This is best ensured by a waterproof strip of asphalt or bitumen, laid over the whole area and extended a short way up any walls or brickwork to prevent water splashes or puddles from soaking into the porous surface.

Roof gardens and balconies rarely suffer from excessive shade, except possibly in highrise blocks, but they are often exposed to intense levels of sunlight, particularly when this is reflected and re-radiated from the surrounding buildings. Also, the higher the roof garden or balcony is, the greater the problems of wind. Wind speed can increase dramatically with fewer obstacles and without filtering plant growth. The problems of funnelling and the build up of speed across the surface of a building can be particularly pronounced.

Both these problems are helped by the construction of pergolas and screens; these should be incorporated into any design to reduce the amount of radiation and cut down the windspeed. Bear in mind, however, that any windshield must be firmly fixed to withstand the strong winds that it will be battling against. Before erecting any structures, be sure to notify any local residents associations and consult the neighbours. A screen will not be popular if it blocks their only direct sunlight.

Considerations of access are probably less important, but if the materials and ornaments needed cannot be carried through the building for reasons of size or weight, they will have to be winched up outside.

The logistics of watering must also be considered. Is hand watering practical? Will time be saved by an automatic irrigation system? If affordable, the automatic system is a good buy as the wind will draw the water from the plants and put them under stress. A semi-automatic system involving an outside tap to which a drip system or 'leaky hose' can be connected and set up to irrigate each pot and container and may be a more practical alternative for a smaller area.

To some extent, plants will be limited in stature by the volume of soil they have to grow in; trees, for example, will be small and of a limited life span. Much of the planting height will have to be achieved through the use of climbers trained up trellises and wires to cover walls and provide screening. The lush green foliage of such plants, combined with bright splashes of colour provided by summer bedding and dwarf bulbs, may be all the planting that is required to transform a stark balcony or roof into a living environment.

Below. *This elegant balcony is brought to life by window boxes filled with strong colours.* Cinerarea *and begonias give most of the effect.*

REFLECTING THE SKY

Blue is not a colour often associated with the garden floor, but with this spacious roof garden it fits the mood perfectly. The choice of colour not only echoes the sky but also tones well with the grey slate roofs beyond. This garden complements, and is complemented by, the

surrounding roofscape so that screening can take on a more decorative role.

White-latticed trelliswork supports a variety of climbing plants along the garden's most open aspect, and right-angled sections protrude into the area, creating a degree of spacial division. They also direct the eye to the seat and the planting arrangement which forms the focal point of the garden. The view is completed by a modest pergola stained to match the timber decked floor.

The diagonal lines of the decking effectively lead the eye to the sitting area, cleverly avoiding the overt lengthening or widening effect of lines running along or across the main viewing axis.

The warm, rich colouring of the teak benches and table add greatly to the appeal of the garden and are complemented by terracotta pots. Planting is restricted mainly to narrow troughs, placed adjacent to the white trellis on one side and mounted on the low parapet wall elsewhere. Above the wall, black railings add to the security of the area without encroaching into the design.

The calm restful air of the garden is enhanced by the restrained use of colour in the planting. Grey foliage features predominantly and includes border pinks (*Dianthus*), *Santolina* and the tall spikes of *Verbascum*. Flowers are mainly white with the occasional splash of pale pink and yellow to provide points of interest.

The relaxed atmosphere of this garden has been carefully created; a possible addition of a wide shallow pool with a still surface might continue the reflective qualities of the garden. Fountains, low enough to remain unaffected by wind, could be set into action during the evening when entertaining guests.

A much stronger and visually longer vista could be created by altering the angle of the decking and adding a focal point mask fountain on an arched wall and backed by a mirror and trellis. The angle of the mirror should be carefully offset to prevent the onlooker being directly reflected. The two outstanding sections of trellis would be realigned, in this example, and a short walk through a pergola added to retain the feeling of height.

Opposite page. *The linear form of the planting lends itself to a simple irrigation system of 'leaky' hoses laid on the surface of the soil.*

Left. *By off-setting the pool in the circular area of decking, any feeling of formality is prevented from creeping into the layout.*

Below. *The inclusion of a mirror behind the focal point fountain can effectively double the apparent length of the vista.*

A SUMMER PARADISE

Timber slats form a partial ceiling to this sunbaked balcony and throws a rigid pattern of shadows over the timber-clad floor. The use of naturally stained timber continues in the wooden balustrade and built-in bench seats; it is therefore by far the most important element in the design.

The planting is limited, and is restricted to a collection of pots and a number of hanging and wall-mounted baskets. Instead, interest is focused on the countryside which surrounds the balcony on three sides. The pots and baskets serve only to bring its greenness into the garden area.

Apart from providing a pleasant, airy environment for eating and relaxing, the balcony is an unusual site for a jacuzzi pool which nestles snugly in one corner surrounded by many of the pots and baskets. When not in use, clean, clear water provides the tub with pond-like qualities, reflecting the greenery that surrounds it. Here, a more solid balustrade supports the wind-reducing slatted side screen to form a protected area for bathing.

The neutral colours in use on the balcony help to stray further into the countryside beyond. Only the bright yellow fabric used for

Below. *The translucent cloth of roller blinds would provide a more even shade that might be gentler on the eye.*

Right. *The slatted roof creates a strong pattern of sun and shade which throws the table and chairs into sharp relief. The use of hanging baskets keeps much of the floorspace free of obstruction.*

cushions on the seats around the table interrupts that, helping to balance the comparative weight of the jacuzzi area. The effect could be softened by draped sheets of neutrally coloured cloth. The heavy canvas of sailcloth would be particularly suitable and its off-white colour would blend well with the other features. This could be lashed to the crossbeams already included in the design but would have to be removed during periods of unsettled weather.

Easier to remove would be roller blinds of the same neutral colour. These could be fixed behind the built-in seats to the rear of the balcony and, when drawn, would loop between the beams to be fixed on the opposite side.

Below. *The soft arching leaves of* Chlorophytum *mask the sharp angles of the benched surround to the jacuzzi and help to create a more private enclosure.*

A LAWN ON THE ROOF

Below. *Layout plan. Key: a) planting; b) artificial grass; c) trough); d) timber decking; e) feature area; f) pots; g) a timber pergola could be added overhead at this point.*

One of the few problems of roof and balcony gardens is that they are almost always architectural in style — directly related to the restrictions and influences of a site and its surroundings.

This clever roof garden manages to break away from the norm by having much of its area covered by a lush green lawn. On first inspection, this might seem almost impossible: the soil requirement and necessary maintenance, linked with poor access, make it extremely difficult to maintain. But closer inspection reveals the garden's secret — artificial turf!

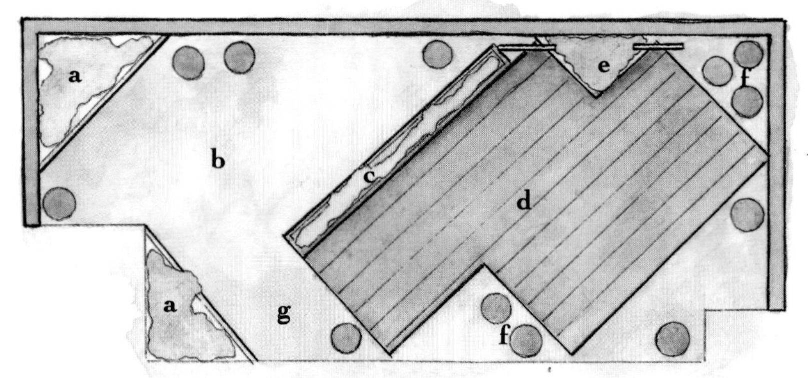

Below. *Dark strap-like leaves are contrasted against the silvery filigree of* Artemisia *and the grey-green mounds and yellow flowers of* Helianthemum *to create the garden's main focal point.*

While most artificial grass mats would be too bright or coarse to combine visually with a garden scene, this careful selection of a dull green colour and a close, even texture for the grass mat has led to as close a mimic of natural turf as could be desired.

The raised dais of decking, which doubles as the main seating area, provides a change in levels. The timber boards are stained a dull mid-brown, and tone well with the brickwork of this and surrounding buildings. They also make a mellow background against which the brighter hues of the planting can be viewed. By setting the wooden platform at an angle, triangular areas have been created adjacent to the building and parapet wall. These have been partly filled with pea-shingle to provide a welcome contrast in texture and an ideal foil for the low, mounding plants.

The wide timber trough built in conjunction with the decking hosts a rich variety of plants with arching sprays of the yellow flowered *Genista lydia* contrasted with *Rosmarinus officinalis, Senecio greyi* and the strong, spiky *Cordyline australis*. This band of planting helps to visually break up the area, separating the raised timber area from the lawn.

Where the decking joins the parapet wall a sturdy timber handrail provides a necessary degree of safety. A central break in the handrail frames the main focal point of the garden — a raised timber bed holding a bold grouping of

plants. A collection of terracotta and black glazed plots repeat throughout the design, giving a sense of continuity to the roof garden.

Should more height be required in the garden, the use of a simple wooden pergola could be considered. Relatively light timbers would be used in the construction to prevent imbalance in the overall design; by using the same brown satin, continuity would be ensured. The pergola would continue the same angled theme as the decking and would increase a spacial division within the garden. This, of course, is provided that the construction of such a structure would be permitted in the area.

The edges of the raised beds and trough could be broadened to provide occasional, informal seating, although such a ploy should not be overplayed for fear of devaluing the impact of the planting.

Above. *Bold foliage groups such as the leathery-leafed* Fatsia japonica, *grey* Euphorbia *and variegated* Euonymus *shown in the foreground give impact to the planting. The* Fatsia *and other plants are repeated in the design to aid continuity in the scheme.*

CHAPTER
SELECTED GARDENS
SEVEN

A BACKGROUND OF WHITE

A CLEAN, CRISP LAYOUT has been created in this town garden by drawing it together with white painted boundary walls. The crispness of white paint has been continued through the trellis and pergola arrangement which divides the garden and onto the cast iron steps that lead to the upper ground floor.

The main access to the garden is from the lower ground floor via a conservatory and a flight of quarry-tiled steps. These steps rise between two walls topped with timber troughs filled with a concoction of herbaceous plants, climbers and trailing bedding plants, including the brightly flowered pink verbena.

At the top of the stairs, a broad York stone paved path leads to a secluded sitting area to the rear of the garden. Blue engineering bricks border the flagstones and are continued as a mowing edge around the almost semi-circular lawn. These engineering bricks are extremely hard and will withstand the regular freezing and thawing of winter frost without any sign of shattering. In this garden, their dark blue/grey colour works well with the subtle and varied hues of York stone.

Next to the house, the ground is paved with granite setts, which although a similar colour to

Below. *The white spangled flowers of the planting give the garden grace and elegance.*

Opposite page. *The grey and brown hues of the granite setts help to combine the various elements of the design.*

the York stone, provide an interesting contrast in texture. A collection of pots and tubs, including several filled with small white marguerites daisies, complete the scene.

The trellised screen helps to create a certain period elegance in the garden. This screen crosses the garden, which helps to protect the

Far left. *This modern adaptation of a period feature combines the needs of modern living with a more traditional refinement.*

sitting area beyond while framing views into the area. Each of the white painted posts is topped with a flat cap and small spherical finial. Versailles cases, which have similar finials at the top of each corner, are included and contribute greatly to the style. A standard Portuguese laurel (*Prunus lusitanica*) is a fine specimen in the central bay of the screen: its dark, glossy foliage shows up well against the bright trellis behind.

The theme of white is continued into the planting with standard roses lining the main access path. Blues and pinks are used sparingly to give a very simple and muted colour scheme. The purple leaves of a young copper beech (*Fagus sylvatica* 'Riversii') are welcome in the design and with the occasional stained timber and terracotta features, add a little warmth.

A slightly less formal, but equally elegant, scheme could have been achieved by the omission of the trellis and pergola, and the substitution of a small gazebo-style structure. This would be construced in the corner of the garden and supported by the boundary walls. The surrounding paving area could be raised slightly to give an interesting break in levels, surfaced with granite setts edged with blue engineering bricks, as here, but with bricks set on edge to give a shallow step up. A more random arrangement of pots and tubs could decorate the paving and the same soft planting could be used to complete the picture.

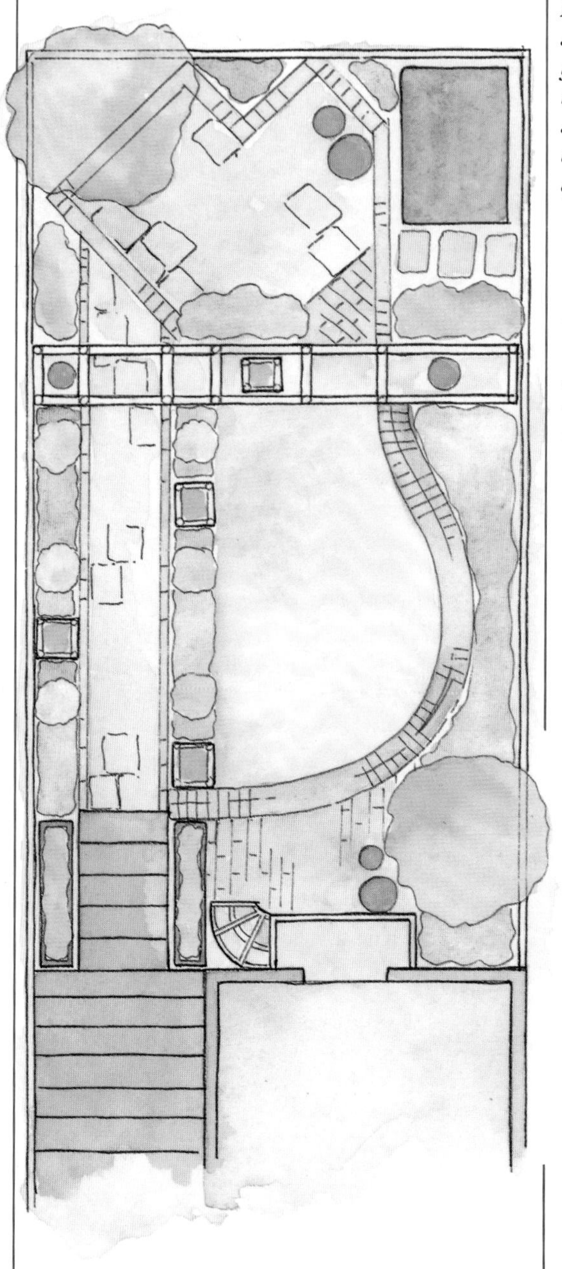

Left. *This illustration shows the layout of the garden but has substituted brick paving for the existing slabs to show how its powers of direction can be put into effect.*

Cottage Charm

An unusual sense of scale prevails in this small front garden; the intimate features of the cottage are almost dwarfed to doll's house proportions. Much of this effect is created by the large water-worn rocks used to edge the borders – their smooth rounded shapes resemble the giant eggs of some prehistoric reptile.

The garden is approached from a country lane through a gateway in an old, moss-covered dry-stone wall. Simple paving of old concrete slabs provides an unobtrusive background to the white rocks and brightly hued planting that hangs over them. The distinctive herringbone folage of *Cotoneaster horizontalis* repeats frequently around the garden, and the dark green leaves of ivy clambering up the house successfully tie it to the garden.

In one corner of the plot a tall cream-coloured chimney pot provides an incidental feature and is surrounded with a mass of bloom provided by double-flowered tuberous begonias. The arching leaves of *Crocosmia* and *Chlorophytum* combine with the ivy covering of an adjacent stump to give a generally weeping nature to the arrangement, helping to retain the eye within the boundaries of this tiny and very colourful garden.

Below. *Key: a) gate; b) old stone wall; c) ivy-covered stump; d) chimney pot; e) background planting; f) large rounded stones; g) doors.*

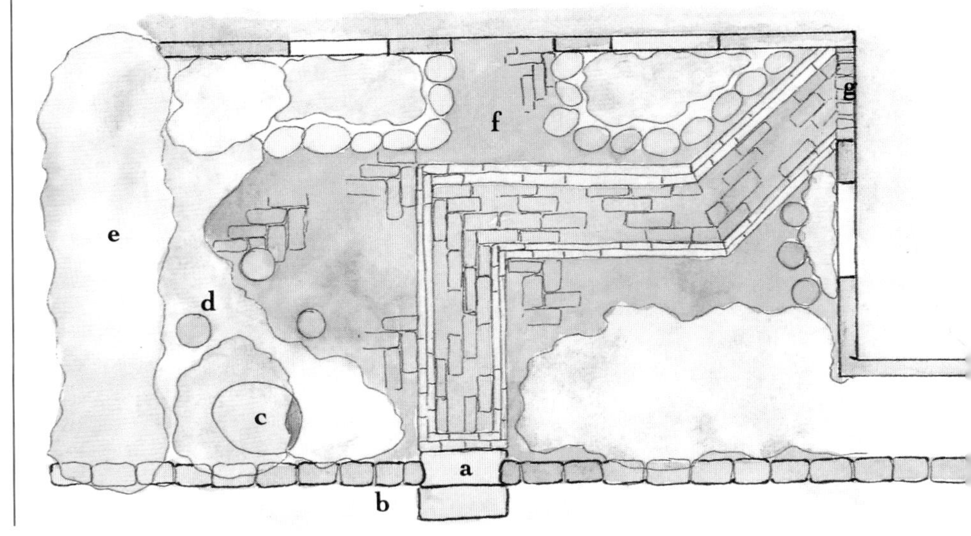

Above. *On entering the garden the eye is immediately drawn to the bold shapes of water-worn rocks that surround the beds adjacent to the house.*

While the planting generally includes a plethora of bright colours, they are almost entirely selected from a limited colour range — yellow through orange to red — so avoiding the jarring effect of clashing colours.

Perhaps the garden's only shortfall is the confusion between two doors that open into the area. The main entrance is hidden from initial view and requires a sharp turn to the right on entering through the gate. Straight ahead, however, is another door intended purely for family use. This rather unusual situation could be partially resolved by introducing a sense of direction into the paving.

Lines of blue engineering brick set level with the paving on either side of the intended walkway could turn to the right to set the visitor on the correct route. The same grey slabs could be re-used or a stronger effect created by substituting old red bricks as the paving medium. By using the stretcher pond pattern within the bands of engineering brick, and perhaps basketweave pattern or herringbone pattern elsewhere, a greater sense of direction could be achieved.

Old stock bricks will weather quickly and the faces of some bricks can be shattered by frost depending on the weather conditions in your area to leave a slightly uneven surface. In this garden the dark colour of moss-covered bricks would throw the rounded stones into much sharper relief and increase their impact.

IMMEDIATE RESULTS

While only recently constructed and planted, this small surburban garden already has a great air of maturity, lent mainly by an old wisteria which has been retrained to give a good degree of cover on the garden's western and southern boundaries.

A single bar pergola has been simply constructed from sawn and treated softwood along the rear boundary; its height and position have been selected to screen overlooking windows from the houses beyond. Vigorous climbers such as *Vitis coignetiae, Clematis montana rubens* and *Lonicera japonica* have quickly scaled the framework, and with the retrained wisteria have given considerable height to the planting in a very short space of time. They provide an excellent display and also effectively screen the necessary windows without using tall fences, which would cut out too much light from this southerly aspect.

The remaining planting is mainly shrubby, which needs little maintenance, with a wide selection of low ground-covering herbaceous plants such as *Ajuga reptans, Campanula poscharskyana* and *Tiarella cordifolia.* The ground cover helps to suppress weeds and provide additional spring and summer colour. Areas of special interest include a small herb area situated close to the kitchen door and a low bed with weathered rocks and a collection of alpines and dwarf conifers. Behind the alpine bed, a short stepping stone path picks its way through low scented mats of thyme and camomile, which give an aromatic walk and easy access to the wide border area.

The paving style has been kept simple and relies on a modern slab with riven surface and

Left. *The large wisteria will be covered in racemes of fragrant mauve flowers during May and June, an impressive element in the garden.*

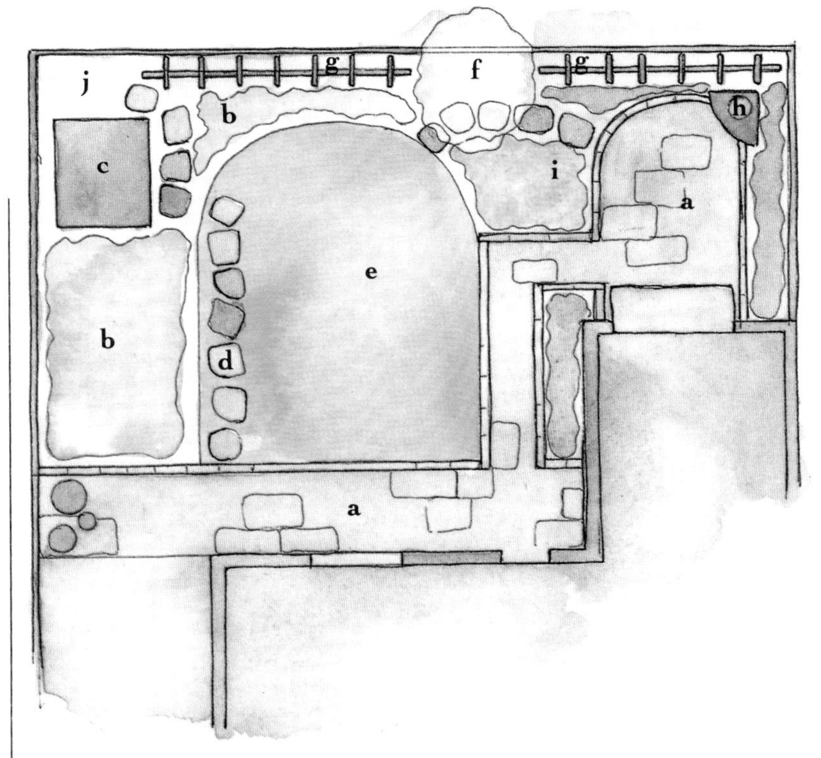

Above. *Plan of area. Key: a) paving; b) planting; c) shed/summerhouse; d) stepping stone path; e) lawn; f) apple tree; g) single-bar pergola; h) feature pot; i) rockery; j) compost/storage.*

weathered grey colour, selected to merge with the yellow stock bricks of the house. The same yellow bricks have been used to give a neat finish to the paving and help unite the house and garden. An interesting shadow line has been created by slightly raising the brick edging; the faces of bricks laid in this manner are also liable to dry more readily, which reduces their susceptibility to frost. It is worth noting, however, that occasional joints in the brickwork must be left unmortared to allow the paving to drain satisfactorily.

A simple arch-shaped lawn combines well with the rectangular shape of the house, introducing bold curves to the garden and giving a pleasant, soft appearance. Unusual pots and artefacts give character to the garden and one of these — an enormous glazed Victorian pot and stand — forms an impressive feature to the terrace area. It is set on a low plinth of brick which highlights its pale creamy colour, and contains a mass of pink verbena.

When the planting has matured, most of the bare walls and fences will be covered with a rich varety of foliage and colours and forms. No doubt there will be scope for additional ornament, perhaps in the form of incidental features set in the planting, if suitable items are found. A small, pale statue or figure could be set behind the alpine bed, forming an excellent focal point to the straight section of path that runs alongside the house.

__Right.__ A simple standard lamp makes an effective focal point against the dark painted walls of the house. The stone steps have mellowed to the point that they appear to have been part of the landscape for many years.

Above. *The two white chairs look back over the lawn from their partly hidden position next to the roses.*

THE COUNTRY RETREAT

This imposing large clapperboard house stands proudly above the lawn and soft planting of this country garden. The dark blue-grey paint enables the building to fade into the scene and prevents it from dominating the area.

Wooden verandas create an easy transition from the house to the garden, and from here steps of random natural stone weave their way down the lawn through a broad expanse of rock and scree garden. The use of several species of low mounding *Helianthemum* and *Phlox douglasii* with soft grey and green foliage and pink and white flowers, contrast with the bolder foliage forms of *Yucca* and *Euphrobia wulfenii* to give a warm, almost Mediterranean feel to this part of the garden.

The broken stones of the steps and path shelter a number of tiny alpines which spread like little rivulets along the cracks. A bold group of the yellow flowered *Alyssum saxatile* are situated at the lowest section of path which joins a lush expanse of green lawn.

A broad band of soft herbaceous planting surrounds the grass, and this, in turn, is supported by a framework of evergreens. Towards the rear of the garden a bed of brightly coloured lupins, backed by topiaried yew, separates a small informal sitting area from the remainder of the garden. Boundary planting and a pergola create an enclave of roses.

Although this garden is larger than many, the same soft planting and country feel could be transferred to a smaller garden with equal success. By screening the boundaries completely, the garden would be effectively removed from its surroundings, which gives the designer a much freer hand with layout and style of planting. Screening can cause a secondary problem of shading in a small garden, but if it is not too dense, careful use of species such as *Alchemilla, Geranium endressii* and *Dicentra* would create the same billowing effect in such conditions. Foxgloves (*Digitalis*) would create the same billowing effect in such conditions. Foxgloves (*Digitalis*) and the annual tobacco plant *Nocotiana* would give added height towards the rear of the border.

A COBBLE BEACH

Below. The young plants leave the layout of the scheme clearly visible, but already the bold leaf shapes add greatly to the various textures of the garden.

The bold architectural planting of this garden sets the mood and defines the spaces within the scheme. From a small paved terrace leading out of a large conservatory, a path of concrete stepping stones set in small, rounded cobbles begins its journey through the garden.

A tall clump of *Miscanthus sacchariflorus* stands proudly in the centre of the garden forming a pivot for the design. Immediately beyond this point the stepping stones reach a wide timber bridge which cuts across the corner of a gently shelving pool. The rounded stones that surround the square concrete slabs of the path slip quietly into the water, forming a cobbled beach — an effect accentuated by the careful placing of water-worn rocks.

The timber bridge extends into a decked sitting area which fills the sunniest part of the garden and forms the remaining boundaries of the pool. Bamboo screens fixed to the boundaries and the brick-built building to the rear of the garden give an essence of Japanese design

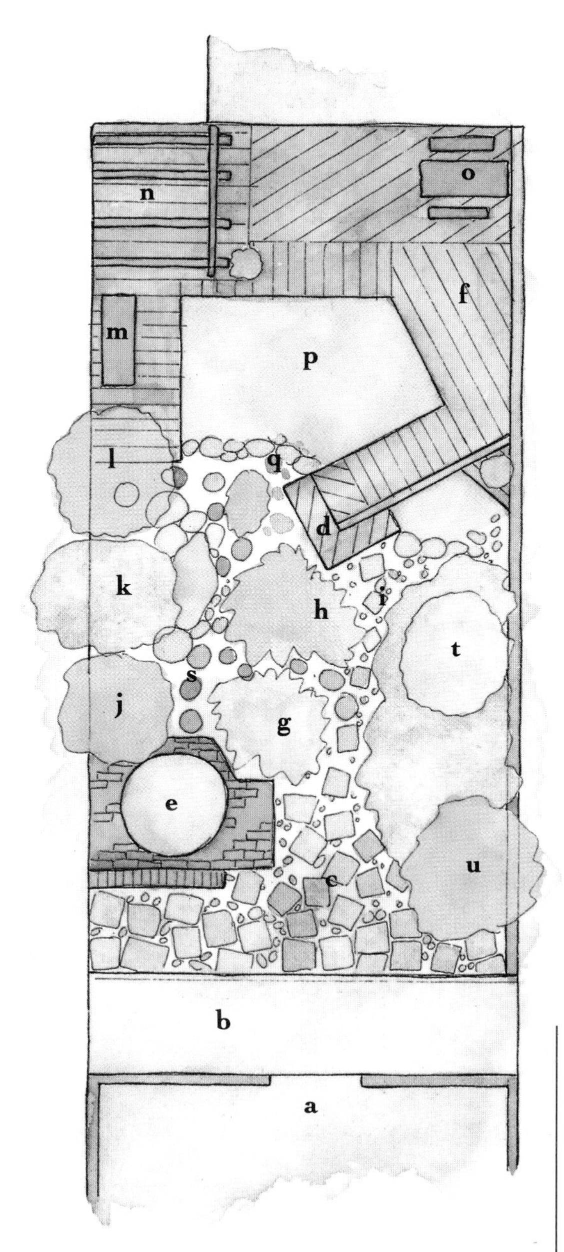

Above. *Plan of area. Key: a) house; b) conservatory; c) terrace of paving slabs and cobbles set in mortar; d) steps; e) hot spa tub; f) timber decking; g)* Yucca; *h)* Miscanthus; *i) stepping stone path; j)* Ligustrum ovalifolium *'Aureum'; k)* Philadelphus; *l)* Pyracantha; *m) bench; n) pergola over; o) table and benches; p) pond; q) cobble 'each; r) rock pool; s) stepping stone path of logs; t) Eucalyptus; u)* Prunus *(flowering cherry).*

Above. *In the more mature planting, the frothy yellow flowers and grey tinged leaves of* Alchemilla mollis *grace the edges of the stepping stone path and offset the long straight leaves of* Miscanthus sacchariflorus *(centre) and* Yucca glauca.

to the bold, simple lines of the area. A timber pergola, strong enough to support a hammock in summer, provides a shady corner for the hottest days of the season.

At the front of the garden, a hidden rock pool is overshadowed by the mature growth of *Philadelphus* and *Pyracantha* retained from the previous layout. It is approached through a jungle of plants by a path formed from short sections of tree trunk. These rise above a thick carpet of weed-suppressing ground covers, complementing the lush growth of ferns and moss in the garden.

A tremendous variation exists in the greens and foliage shapes of the planting, removing the need for much additional colour; occasional splashes of yellow blend well into the scheme, though, and serve to highlight various points along the main parts. In the darkness, strategically placed spotlamps throw light up into the taller plants, highlighting the various textures.

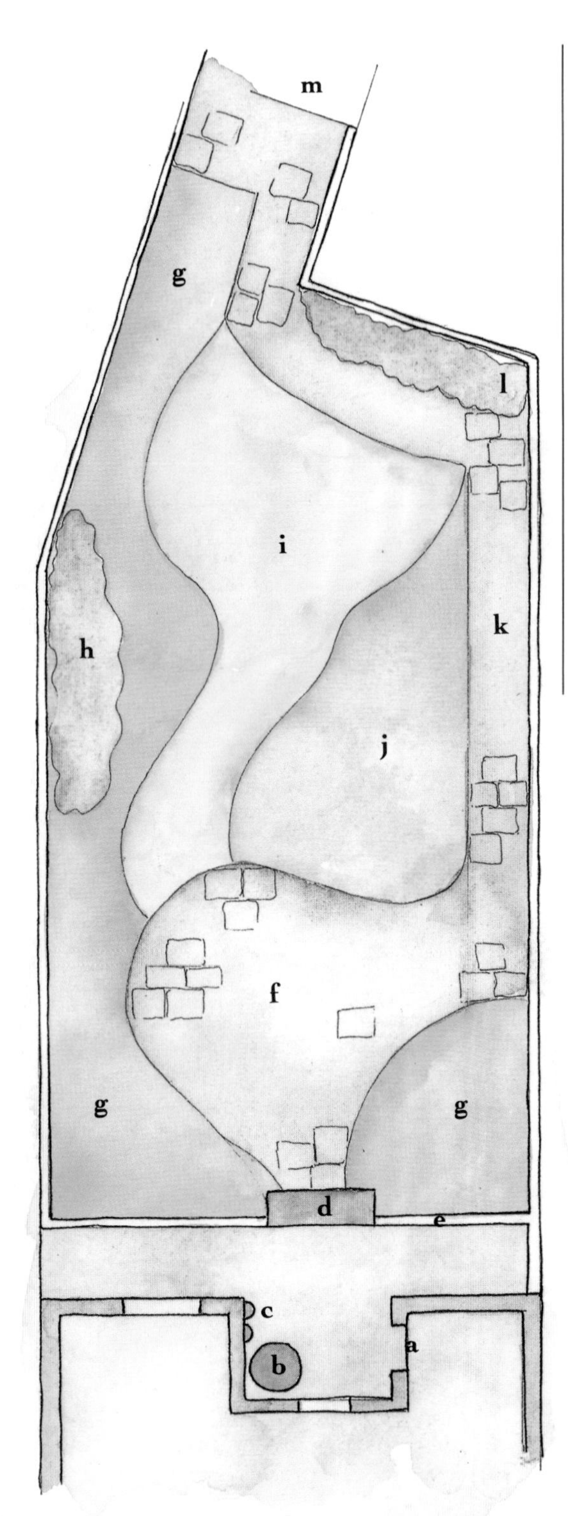

Above. *Plan of area. Key: a) door, b) wash stand; c) terracotta masks; d) archway; e) trellis fence; f) paved terrace; g) planting; h) golden conifers; i) lawn; j) rock garden; k) paved path; l) group of chimney pots; m) storage area and compost.*

POTS AND PLANTS

A love of plants has shaped this garden into an informal layout teeming with life and colour. A particular interest in alpines is satisfied by a large rock garden, with less robust specimens given the safe harbour of pots, tubs and a small sink garden.

The miniature spires and domes of dwarf conifers stand in a patchwork quilt of low-spreading plants on the rockery. The rocks themselves are large enough to hold their own with the planting but are placed carefully and set well in the soil so as not to dominate the whole view.

Across a narrow strip of lawn, larger conifers form a backdrop to a bed of low perennials, including the white flowered *Iberis sempervirens*. An incidental feature is provided by a small

Right. *The old washstand, terracotta masks and pots make an attractive combination.*

Below. Saxifraga, Sempervivium *and dwarf conifers make a miniature landscape in this sink garden. Further pots add to the variety.*

white figurine which is highlighted by the afternoon rays of the sun. Lightweight trellis forms the two main boundaries of the garden, giving an open, spacious feel to the plot and doubling as a support for a wide variety of climbers.

Along one side of the garden a straight, purposeful path is terminated by an informal group of old chimney pots, now used as decorative plant holders. From here, another short path leads on to the partly screened area tucked neatly into one corner for storage and compost.

The imaginative use of all types of containers as plant holders is a strong feature in this garden; even an old bucket has found a new lease of life after receiving a coat of white paint. One such container, an old washstand, forms the main element in a tiny courtyard area in front of the house. In combination with terracotta pots on the ground and on the window sill, the washstand is planted with variegated ivy and brightly flowered geraniums which lighten the area in the summer months. Two terracotta masks hung on a bare white wall receive similar treatment, their ivy and trailing geraniums reaching downwards during the summer until they mingle freely with the planting below.

The intimacy of this area is helped by the climber-covered trellis and archway that separate it from the garden. The archway — positioned centrally to one of the house windows — serves as a frame for views into, and out of, the main area of garden.

While the plain grey paving seen here is unobtrusive, small unit paving could be used to introduce a subtle form of pattern into the area, while keeping the scale of the detailed planting that features so strongly in the design. Old stock bricks for the main paths could be mixed with square granite setts used in random blocks where pots and tubs are to stand — an attractive combination without forcing a modern feel on the garden. The granite setts are less even to walk on and so are better positioned in areas less frequently used. Such small paving elements could also be moulded around the many curves that give the garden its free-flowing form.

A COBBLED COURTYARD

In a hot Mediterranean climate the cool shade of this courtyard gives a welcome reprieve from the mid-day sun. The bare trunk of a pine adds a sculptural element to the garden, and the spread of its canopy adds to the shade cast by the house. A mound of rough, pitted rocks surrounds the base of the tree, which resolves the awkward junction of the trunk with the plane of the terrace.

The same gnarled rocks are repeated around the few borders in the courtyard, holding soil to give a subtle change in levels. Planting is sparse in the garden due to the parched soil, but grey clouds of *Helichrysum* cover most of the borders and tumble down to the cobbled courtyard floor, the main feature of the garden.

The small round stones that make up the floor have been painstakingly laid to form a neat pattern of squares. This has been achieved by setting single rows of stones on edge in evenly spaced lines running across the garden in two directions. The outline squares that result are then filled in with similar stones set flat in a random pattern. Laid in this way, the straight lines can be readily picked out from a less distinguishable background.

Set against the rich and varied texture of the paving, the smooth lines of a simple pre-cast concrete table make a stark contrast. The thin black lines of the surrounding chairs merge more comfortably with the backdrop.

Green foliage from a young tree throws a bright burst of colour into the picture when backlit by the strong sun. A background of fig and olive screens two sides of the garden with mottled green, while the dark shade of tiled cloisters provides a still darker backcloth to the remaining area. Stern, upright bench seats are partially obscured in the shadows.

Simplicity and texture are the keynotes of this garden and while nothing should be done to detract from these, an extra element of ornament may well benefit the design. A pair, group, or even several groups of smooth stone or cream-coloured earthenware pots and urns, arranged around the brick piers of the cloisters, would not encroach on the main view, but add interest and colour to this dark facade.

Left. *Rich greens and the mellow colours of natural stone make a tranquil setting for a cool afternoon. The deep shade of the cloisters houses the dark upright shapes of long bench seats.*

Above. *The addition of pots and urns around the brick piers of the cloisters could add life.*

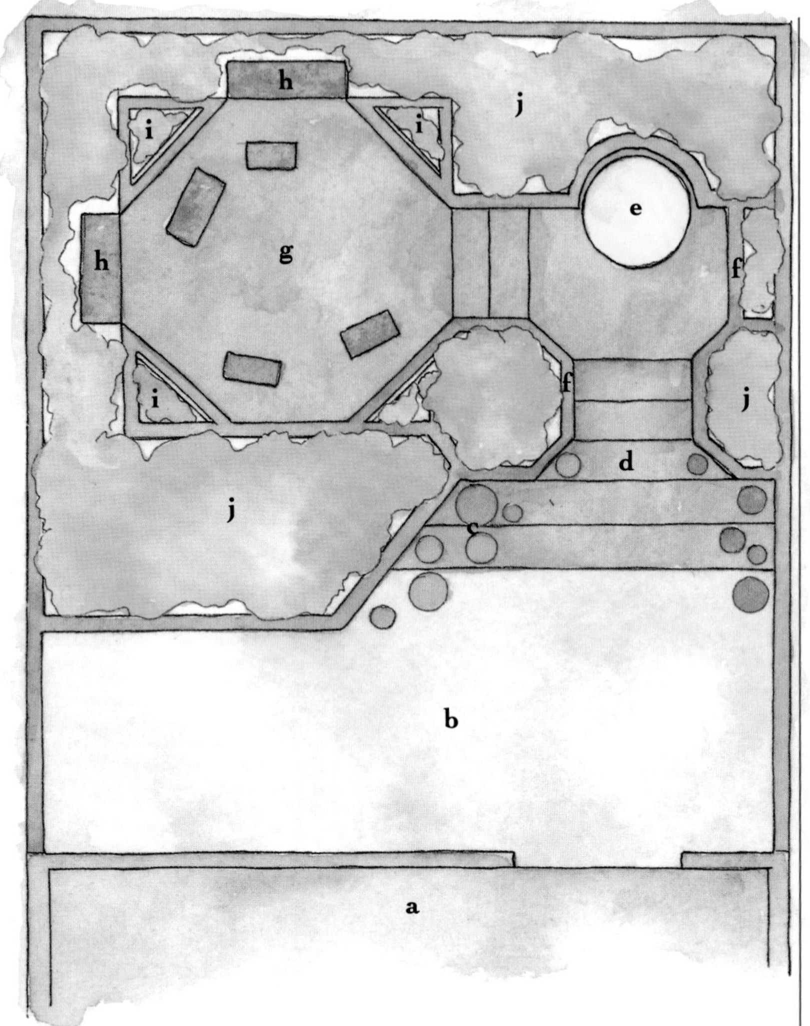

Above. Plan of area. Key: a) house; b) stone paved terrace; c) collection of pots; d) brick steps; e) sand pit; f) retaining walls; g) brick paved upper terrace; h) built in seats; i) raised beds with metal arches over; j) planting.

Opposite page. The split levels of the design divide the garden into separate rooms, making the use of tall planting unnecessary.

Right. Conversion of the circular sandpit to a small format pool in the future would create immediate impact and enliven the area.

PAVED ON TWO LEVELS

The steep drop that runs through this walled town garden helps to sub-divide the area, giving the garden its individuality and its distinctive style.

The sunken area adjacent to the house is paved with large slabs of rectangular York stone, and from here a broad flight of brick paved steps rises between the twin turrets of brick planters. A small circular sandpit backed by a curved wall lies on the central axis of the steps and its possible later conversion to a small formal pool, perhaps with a fountain, would create a well-defined focal point for the area.

The brick paving continues up another two steps into a large octagonal sitting area bounded on alternate facets by tall metal arches. These four arches each support a pair of climbers, giving added height and scale to the area. A lush band of planting wraps around the area and evergreen climbers weave their way up the white walls to the tall trellis that helps isolate the garden from its city surroundings.

The borders carry a rich variety of leaf shapes which include the broad blue leaves of *Hosta sieboldiana,* the glossy green of *Choisya ternata* and the tiny leaves of *Cotoneaster microphyllus.* In brighter areas *Hebe* and lavender can be found.

A selection of teak furniture, both free-standing and built-in, remains as a permanent fixture in the garden, which allows the owners to take advantage of even relatively short spells of good weather throughout the year. An annual oiling of the wood keeps it protected against the rigours of the winter.

The mainly terracotta pots and tubs accommodate a variety of foliage plants and brightly flowering annuals. The soft grey spreading foliage of *Helichrysum petiolatum* is used throughout the design, and particularly next to the broad brick steps where pots of white flowered *Impatiens* line the walls.

The repetition of shapes and angles gives the overall design a pronounced sense of unity. Note especially how the octagonal shape of the main sitting area reappears in the brick planters by the steps and is partially repeated in the lower paving. Coping bricks with a single cant (angled corner) echo the theme on the internal walls.

FREE-FLOWING GRAVEL

Heavy blocks of planting successfully break the length of this narrow garden, throwing the path from side to side so that a direct view from one end to the other is continually avoided.

The lush green planting nearest the house is punctured with bright yellow flowers which compete happily with the bold foliage for attention. The thin and strap-like leaves of *Hemerocallis* and the spiky *Verbascum* and *Eremurus* rise distinctly above the billowing mass of supporting plants. A collection of low pots and bowls enables the planting to spill out onto the terrace and small groups of rounded cobbles help blend the various elements.

This first expanse of lower planting is balanced by a narrower but much taller group further down the garden, giving a tremendous sense of dynamic movement to the design.

Around these two blocks of green winds a path of small beige pebbles contained by brick on either side. This eventually arrives at a partially hidden area with large stone slabs set like dark islands in a sea of white quartz chippings. The gradual colour transformation of the stone chippings is almost indiscernible; only when the white stones light up the area of shade is the change confirmed.

The garden is bounded by tall creeper-clad walls which provide a high degree of seclusion and security. At the end of the garden, screens of bamboo canes lashed to a timber framework are substituted for the brickwork, which accentuates the area's more oriental feel.

Although there are no internal structures within the garden, tall trees immediately beyond the far boundary give necessary height to the design.

If a greater degree of enclosure was desired, a short pergola of steel arches could be installed over the main path. This would produce a wonderful progression from light, through shade and back into light as one walked down the garden.

The nodding yellow flowers and silky seed heads of *Clematis tangutica* and the bold leaves and rich autumn colour of *Vitis coignetiae* would be ideal to scramble over the framework of steel and wire.

Above. *The timber-decked terrace directs the eye and the observer along the wide gravel path leading into the distance. Patterns of light and dark are created along the length of the garden by the dappled shade of trees and the contrast of stone and gravel.*

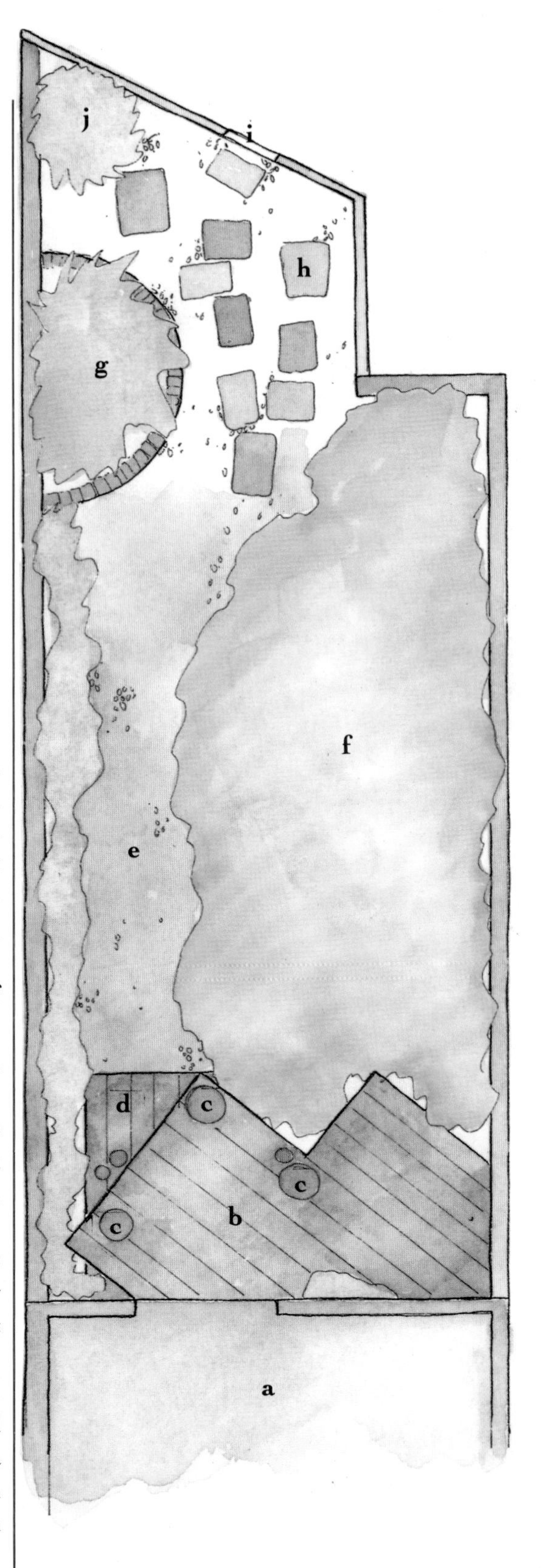

Above. *Plan of the area. Key: a) house; b) timber decking; c) pots; d) steps; e) beige-coloured shingle; f) main body of planting; g) tall planting; h) large stone slabs set in white shingle; i) gate; j) large bamboo.*

Above. *Careful planting in pastel shades and a wonderfully detailed terrace create a delightful garden.*

A THREE-TIERED POOL

It is the sound of water falling from pool to pool that immediately attracts the attention when entering this delightful garden. The softness of the planting, use of bold textures and an ornate trellis screen all combine to give it great style, and a satisfying view from the terrace.

The naturally sloping site has been partially levelled to introduce steps and a series of low walls. This change in levels has been further utilized in the formation of the three formal pools arranged on the terrace. From the upper pool water tumbles from a narrow tile shoot and cascades over a mound of cobbles to the pool below. The effect is repeated from the middle to lower pools, from where a small circulating pump returns it to its source.

Several terracotta pots and tubs contain herbs for use in the kitchen, and the hard lines of the brick are blended into the planting with the soft grey leaves of *Helichrysum petiolatum* and *Stachys olympica.*

From the top of the steps a narrow strip of grass leads to an open lawn and directs the eye to a bold foliage grouping in the opposite corner. Between the trellis screen and a tall privet hedge a sloping gravel path gives wheeled access between the various levels of the garden. The trellis returns across the garden to screen vegetable plots and a play area beyond. A central gap in the trellis aligned with the kitchen window frames a strong vista to a large urn placed at the far end of the plot.

The garden shows how well an interest in gardening can be combined with the needs of a

Below. *Soft planting abounds in the front garden. Here* Cotoneaster salicifolius *'Repens' and rose 'Raubritter' smother a steep bank.*

young family. The lawn and play equipment give ample scope for the more active pursuits of children while the sloped access path doubles as a much-used cycle track. Safety is obviously of paramount importance in the garden and close inspection of the pools reveals a strong metal grid supported just below the surface by pillars of brick.

The use of colour in the garden shows much thought; mellow bricks and the weathered tones of riven paving mingle easily with the varied hues of the planting. The foaming yellow flowers of *Alchemilla* accentuate the lime green tones of the lawn and the mid-brown trellis cuts easily through the garden.

The more open style of garden displayed here is most suitable in a country setting bringing the sights and sounds of the surroundings into the garden. Although the same basic design would work equally well in a town garden, an added element of height would help in screening. The bright yellow green foliage of the tree *Robina pseodoacacia* 'Frisia' would combine easily into the scheme, perhaps near the corner of the trellis where it would echo the *Alchemilla*. A single or double bar pergola running across the garden behind the trellis could continue at the height of the privet hedges, giving a greater degree of seclusion to the lawn area.

Above. *The ornate stonework of the fountain in sharp contrast with the modern lines of house and garden.*

Abstract in Green

A more restrained colour scheme would be harder to imagine than the dark green of evergreen foliage and the warm, rustic tones of brick and terracotta used here.

The garden relies mainly on the strict architectural form of clipped box viewed against the mottled background of brick. The brick paving has a relatively fine pattern which suits the narrow confines of the area and its colour matches the walls and terracotta pots — a major feature in the design — to give a very mellow effect.

The design is formalized around the entrance to the house: low rectangular hedges of box set in brick planters and half-standard specimen plants in terracotta pots. From here, a shallow flight of steps descends to the main area accompanied by a pair of painted stone plinths and finials set like sentinels by the lowest step.

A stone fountain and pool forms the centrepiece of the garden, but is set to one side of the main axis. This allows the eye to continue uninterrupted to an inspired and dynamic abstract of low box spheres and towering, spire-like conifers. At the furthest point, a dark hollow in the wall houses a timber gate, approached by another short flight of steps.

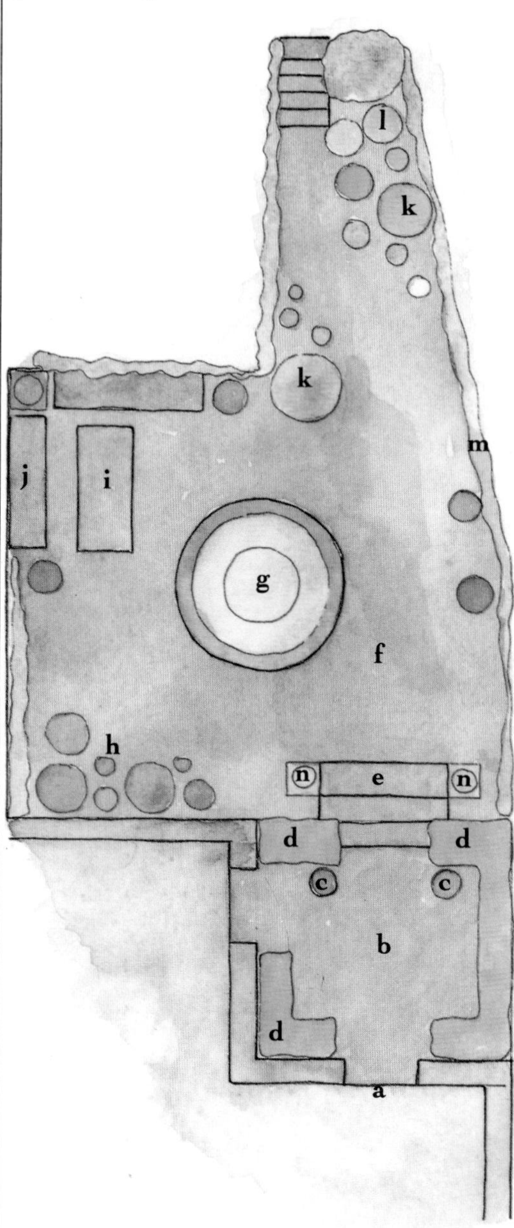

Back in the main area, tall ivy-clad walls shelter built-in benches and a low table. These too are accompanied by clipped box and terracotta. Another corner holds a collection of pots with much softer deciduous planting, hidden from the house to avoid diluting or confusing the pictorial quality.

Two slender storks are set by the pool and fountain; when in use the fountain brings movement into the garden, and when still, birds use the shallow bowl to splash and bathe. The smooth untroubled surface of the pond supports the round, flat leaves of water lillies which will show their elegant blooms in the summer. A ring of tightly-clipped ivy surrounds the pool, lifting it from the paving and masking any uneven edges.

Movement is instilled into the design by the almost surreal shapes of moulded evergreens, which removes the need for additional colour or planting. Any such clutter would serve only to destroy the very simplicity that is the essence of this garden's charm.

Far right. *Lines running through the paving and the progression of clipped box and terracotta pots draw the eye to the focal point of spire-like conifers.*

Right. *Plan of the area. Key: a) doors; b) upper paved area; c) half standard specimens in pots; d) clipped box hedges; e) steps; f) brick paving; g) fountain and pool; h) pots and tubs; i) table; j) built in seats; k) clipped box spheres in terracotta pots; l) conifers; m) climbers on walls; n) piers with spherical finials.*

Glossary

aggregate — Collection of small stone chippings of various sizes, the smaller chippings being small enough to fill the spaces between the larger chippings, so making a more compact surface.

base lines — A long straight line from which shorter measurements may be taken. Used particularly when surveying by triangulation, where measurements are taken from either end of the base line to a third point which is to be fixed. This in effect forms a triangle of which the original line is the base (*see* **offsets**).

batter — When the faces of a wall are built out of the vertical. A free-standing wall built with a batter will have a narrow top and wide base. A retaining wall will effectively lean back against the body of soil being supported.

bull-nosed brick — A specially shaped brick where the angle between stretcher (long, narrow) and header (end) faces is replaced with a radius curve. A double bull-nosed brick will have both the angles on one stretcher face replaced by curves.

cant brick — A specially shaped brick where the angle between stretcher and header faces has effectively been removed to give a new face at 45° to the original two.

chain link — A type of fence formed from thick wires which run from top to bottom and are coupled together to form a continuous net which is then held taut between posts and horizontal wires.

coping — The top layer of wall which is designed to prevent water soaking into the body of the wall.

cord wood — Straight lengths of timber as cut from a tree which are generally quite small in cross section and may be used to retain the sides of a loose laid path.

coursed wall — A wall built in a number of layers which may, or may not, be equal and level, depending on the material used.

edging board — Thin sections of sawn timber normally around 5 in/12.5 cm x 1 in/2.5 cm which has been treated and may be fixed to short timber posts to retain a loose surface. The posts are normally driven to the point where their tops are level with, or below the top of the board, so creating a neat and tidy finish.

granite setts — Blocks of stone that may be either square or rectangular, normally in the 4 in/10 cm to 6 in/15 cm size range and grey, grey-brown or grey-pink in colour.

hardcore — Any of a number of materials such as broken bricks or concrete which can be compacted down to make a solid sub-base on which a concrete or other base can be laid.

in-situ concrete — Concrete that is laid wet and allowed to set in position in which it is to remain, particularly as the finished surface of paths or patios.

jump blocks — Larger blocks of stone or similar, which when used in the construction of a wall are two or more courses high.

offsets — Shorter measurements taken perpendicularly from a longer base line; used when surveying.

pales — Pointed wooden stakes or narrow timber boards fixed to horizontal rails or wires to make a fence.

planting mulch — A layer of peat, bark granules, gravel or similar material spread over the soil surface after planting to help conserve moisture and suppress weeds.

plinth bricks — Specially shaped bricks where one stretcher (long, narrow) face has been effectively cut away at an angle so the top of the brick is narrower than the base. These bricks are used to reduce the width of a wall and give a pleasing sloped edge.

raceme — An inflorescence in which the individual flowers are borne on short stalks around and along the main flower stem, forming a cone of flowers.

reinforcing — A system of using steel bars or mesh in the construction of walls or concrete bases for greater strength.

render — To cover brick or stonework with a layer of cement mortar or similar material.

riven surface — An uneven surface modelled on that of freshly quarried stone.

soakaway — A large pit filled with free-draining material which will collect water and allow it to displace slowly into the ground.

stretcher bond — The simplest pattern in which to lay bricks where a single line of bricks is laid so that the joints come exactly half way along the bricks laid adjacently or in the course below.

timber decking — A layer of wooden boards supported above the underlying ground level on a timber framework.

turves — Shallow strips of grass-covered soil which are used to form an 'instant' lawn.

Versailles case — A square timber plant container on short legs in the style first seen at Versailles in France.

wattle fence — A fence formed from panels made by interweaving twigs or flexible timber rods.

Index

WHY IT WORKS

Most materials have elasticity – they can resume their shape after being squashed. In a spring at rest (1), all the forces acting on it are balanced. Squeezing increases the forces that make the spring want to spring apart (2). Releasing the spring causes it to push apart again.

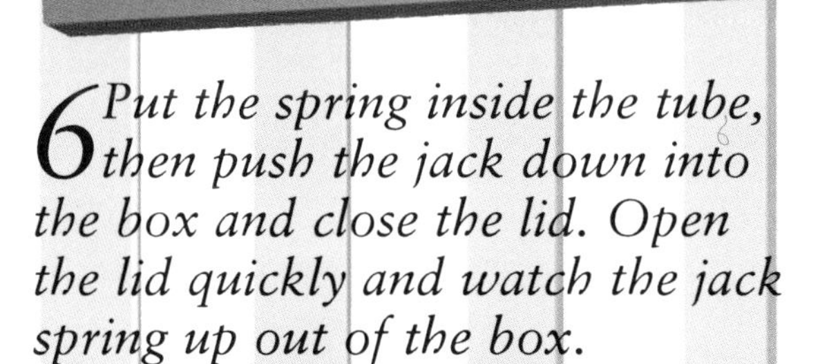

HANGING DOWN

Fix a weight to the end of a ruler. Hang it over the edge of a table. Now move the ruler so it hangs further over the edge. Does it bend more?

6 Put the spring inside the tube, then push the jack down into the box and close the lid. Open the lid quickly and watch the jack spring up out of the box.

MAKING PLASTICS

WHAT YOU NEED
Milk
Saucepan
Vinegar
Paints
Wooden spoon

THE LAST PROJECT SHOWED you how to make metal wire elastic by coiling it into a spring. But some substances do not return to their original shape when pulled out of it. These are plastic substances. Wet clay is plastic because you can mould it into any shape and it stays that way. This project shows how you can turn everyday ingredients into a plastic material.

PLASTIC POT

Place a plastic yoghurt pot in a saucepan. Ask an adult to pour boiling water over it. Watch as it loses its shape.

PLASTIC MILK

1 Ask an adult to slowly warm some milk in a saucepan.

2 Just as the milk is starting to bubble, slowly stir in some vinegar.

WHY IT WORKS

When the vinegar is added to the milk, it starts a chemical reaction. This causes the tiny molecules that make up the milk to clump together. Instead of being runny and free to move, as they are in the liquid milk, the molecules form one large lump. This lump is your plastic material.

MILK MOLECULES
CLUMP TOGETHER

3 *Keep stirring and adding vinegar. Within a few seconds the mixture should turn rubbery.*

6 *Decorate your plastic with paints.*

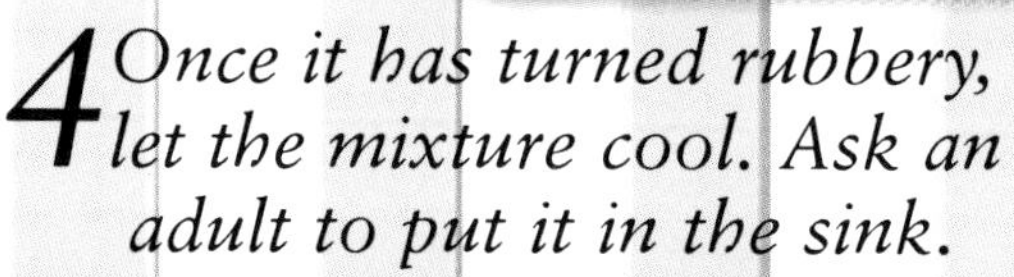

4 *Once it has turned rubbery, let the mixture cool. Ask an adult to put it in the sink.*

5 *Ask an adult to put some of the cooled mixture on a plate. Run it under cold water until it is completely cold.*

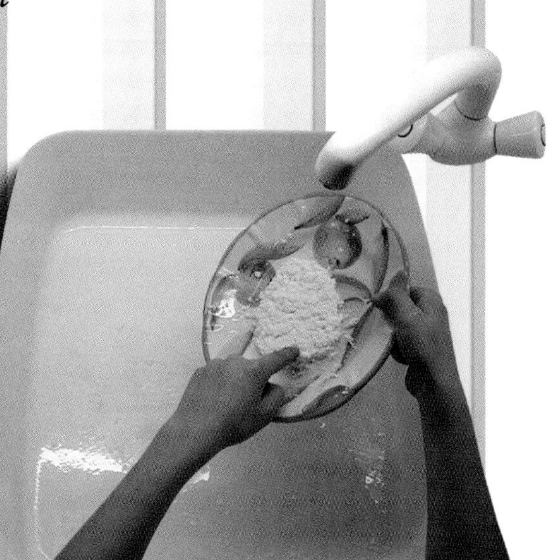

SHAPING MATERIALS

WHAT YOU NEED
Thick card
Sticky tape
Scissors
Modelling clay
Washing-up liquid
Plaster of Paris

PLASTIC MATERIALS CAN CHANGE SHAPE without returning to their original structure, as you saw when you made a plastic substance in the last project. Plaster of Paris is a substance that can take on the shape of any container or mould it is poured into. It starts as a powder-like substance that can be mixed with water to form a paste. The paste then sets hard. This project shows you how to mould plaster of Paris.

MOULDING SHAPES

1 Ask an adult to make a frame out of thick card. Tape it to another piece of card, as shown here. Make a pattern out of modelling clay in the base of your frame.

2 Cover the modelling clay shape with washing-up liquid. This will stop the plaster of Paris from sticking to the modelling clay.

3 Mix the plaster of Paris with some water and pour this into the mould.

4 Cover the modelling clay completely and leave the plaster to harden.

WHY IT WORKS

When plaster of Paris is mixed with water, it forms a paste which can be poured into a mould. Over time, the water evaporates (goes off into the air as a gas) and the paste hardens to form a brittle substance.

PLASTER OF PARIS

WATER

PLASTER PICTURES

Use your mould to make shapes from modelling clay. Simply press the clay into the plaster and it will take on the pattern of the mould.

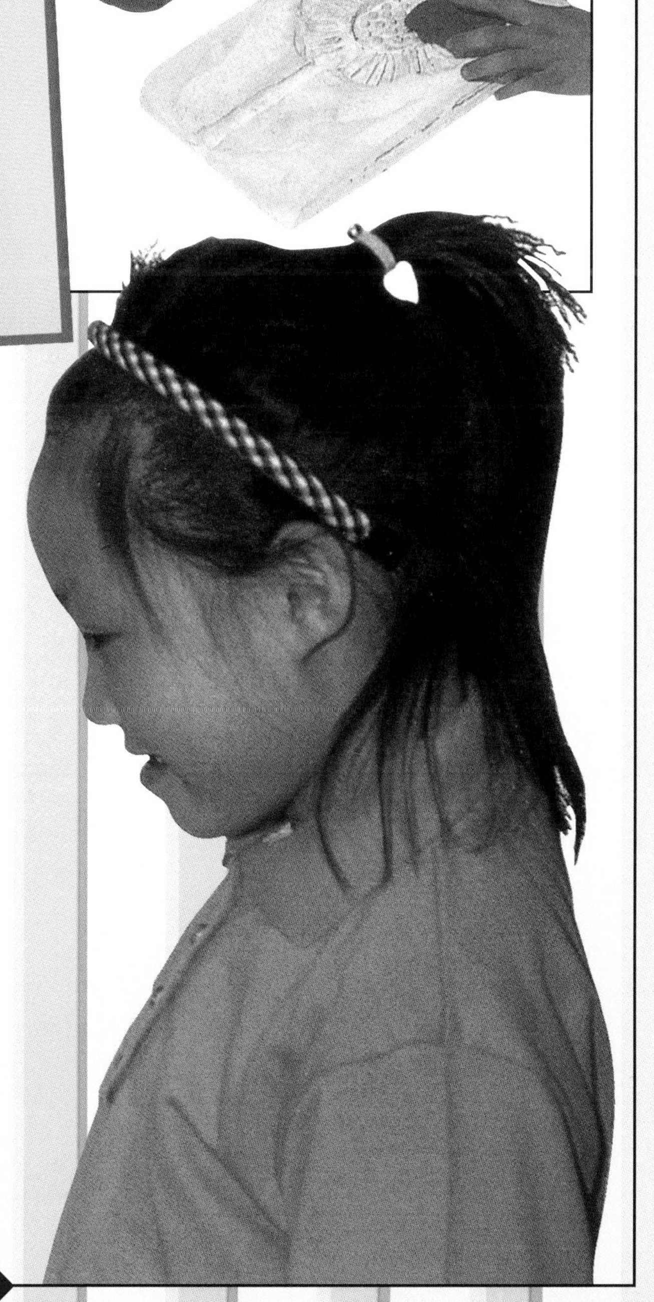

5 When the plaster is dry, gently remove it from the frame. You will see that the plaster has hardened with the shape of the modelling clay set into it.

WHAT YOU NEED
Thick card
Scissors
String
Coloured wool
Wooden dowels

WEAVING MATERIALS

SOME MATERIALS ARE ONLY strong in one direction and are not good on their own for using in structures. One way around this weakness is to weave strands of material together. This creates a new structure which uses its strengths in all directions. Clothing fibres are an example of this. They combine threads to create usable materials. Learn how to weave strands of wool in this project.

WHY IT WORKS

The strings running up and down your loom are called warp threads. The wool strands which you weave across the loom are called weft threads. By weaving the threads together, the finished fabric is strong. The closer the weave, the stronger the fabric.

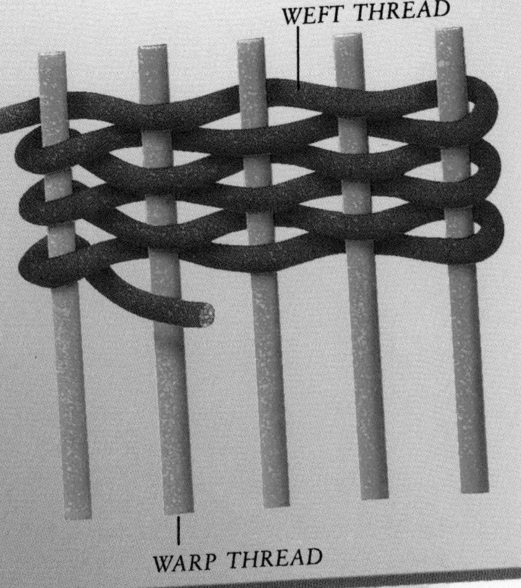

SMOOTH FIBRES

Have a look at the ends of different threads of material with a magnifying glass. Compare the sizes of each fibre and see how smooth the ends are.

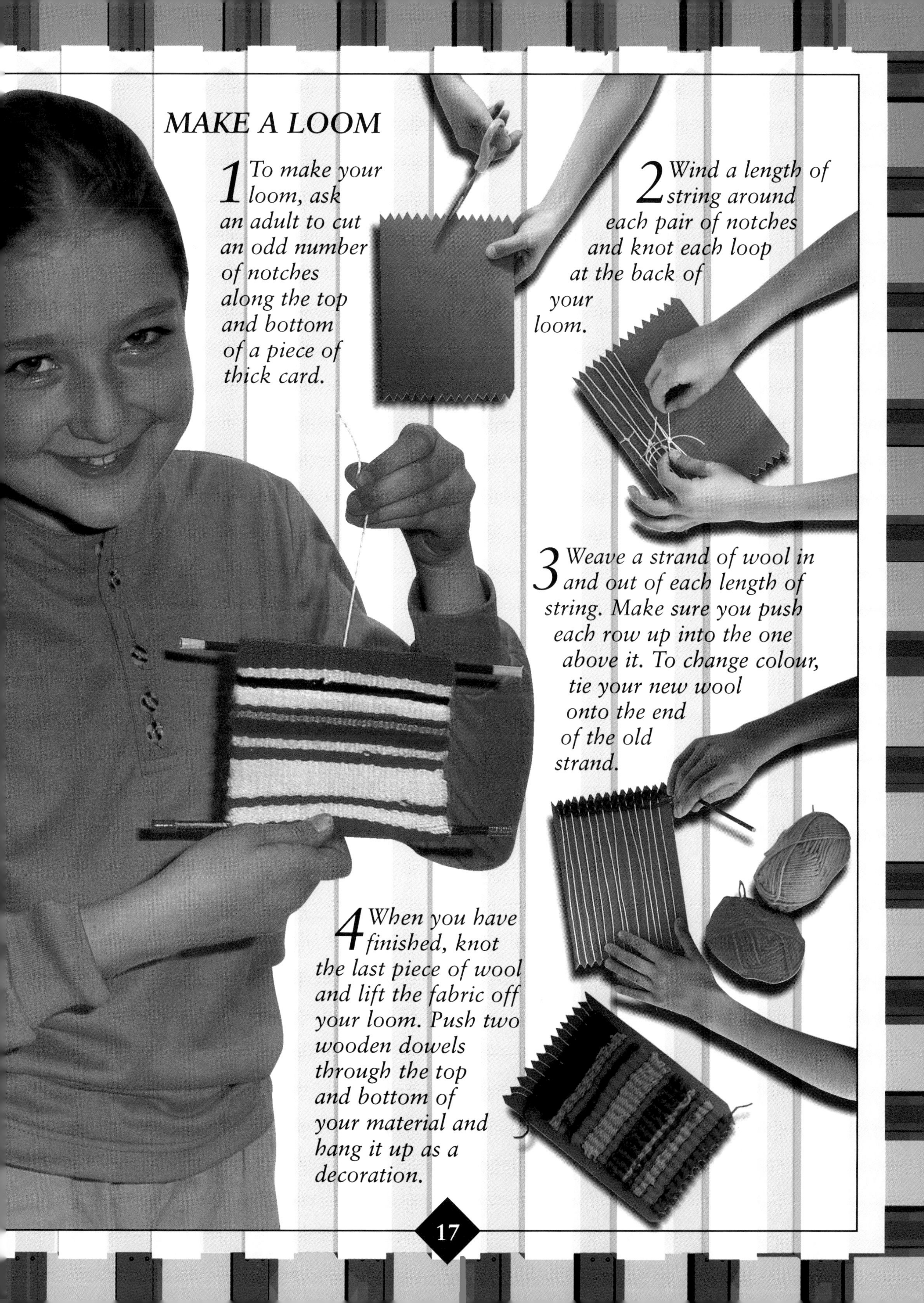

MAKE A LOOM

1 To make your loom, ask an adult to cut an odd number of notches along the top and bottom of a piece of thick card.

2 Wind a length of string around each pair of notches and knot each loop at the back of your loom.

3 Weave a strand of wool in and out of each length of string. Make sure you push each row up into the one above it. To change colour, tie your new wool onto the end of the old strand.

4 When you have finished, knot the last piece of wool and lift the fabric off your loom. Push two wooden dowels through the top and bottom of your material and hang it up as a decoration.

GETTING STRONGER

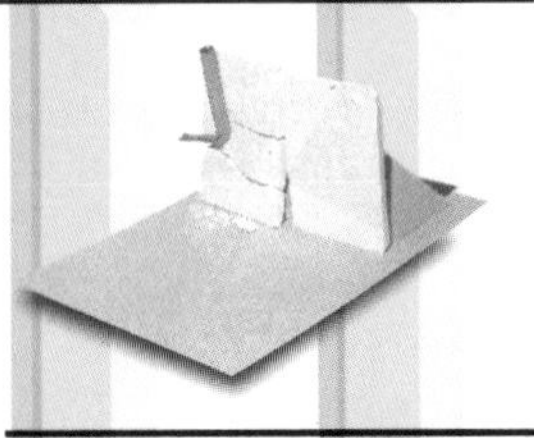

WHAT YOU NEED
Cardboard
Sticky tape
Stiff wire
Plaster of Paris
Weight
String
Scissors
Sheet of plastic

SOMETIMES ONE MATERIAL ON ITS OWN is not suitable for a job, and two or more different materials may need to be combined to create the right material. Fibreglass, for example, contains tiny pieces of glass in a plastic, which makes it both flexible and strong. In this project, see how you can strengthen plaster of Paris by adding another material.

WHY IT WORKS

The block of plaster alone (1) is brittle and will break when a strong force is applied to it. The block that contains the metal wire (2) will last longer because it can bend a little and absorb the knocks it receives.

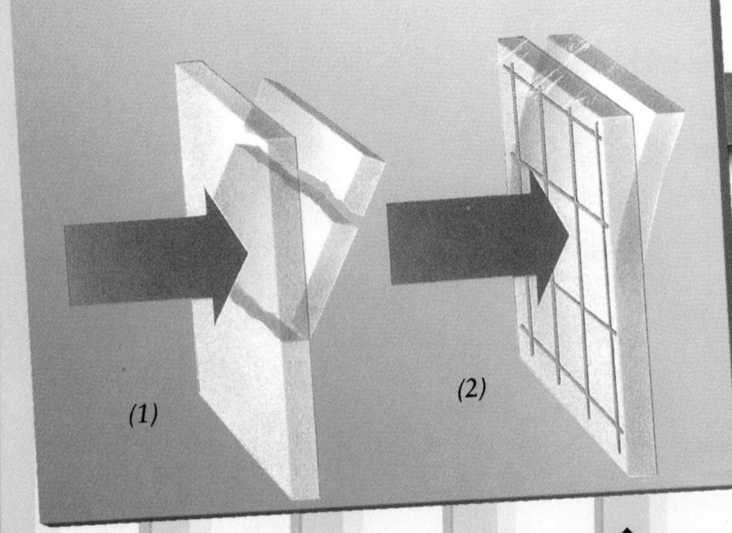

REINFORCED PLASTER

1 Use the frame you made and follow the steps on page 14 to make one block of plaster of Paris. (You don't need to make the mould.)

2 When the block is dry, remove it from the frame. You need to make another block the same size, but before you start, lay some pieces of wire into the frame.

CLAY BRICKS

Make bricks out of clay and leave them to harden. Now make more bricks of the same size, but this time mix some straw into the clay. Test them for strength and find out which ones last the longest.

5 Swing the weight at the blocks of plaster. Make sure that you hit each block at the same spot and that you release the weight from the same distance each time.

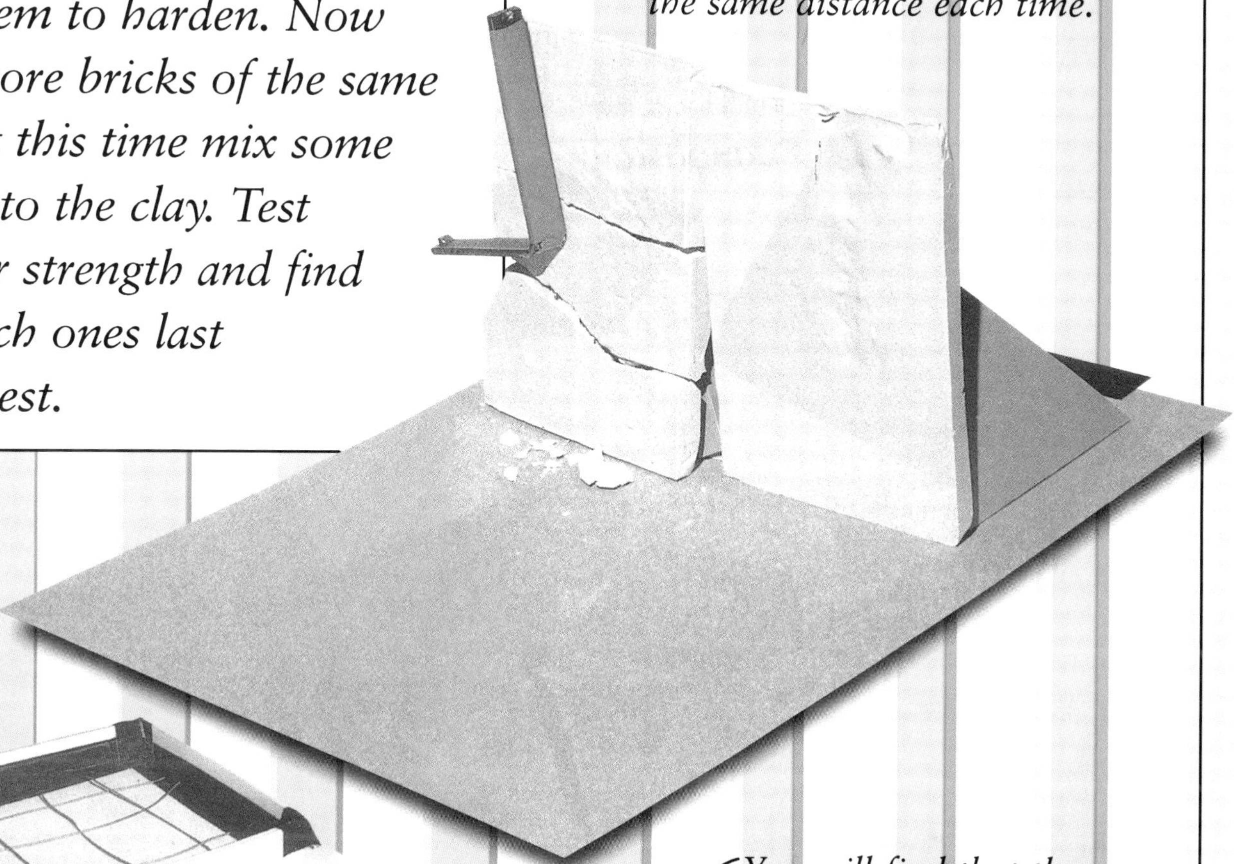

3 Lay the wires both across and lengthways, as shown here. Now make your second block of plaster with the wires embedded in it.

4 Ask an adult to cut out cardboard supports. Lean the blocks against these on a sheet of plastic, as shown. Tie a weight to a length of string. Tie up the string so that it can swing.

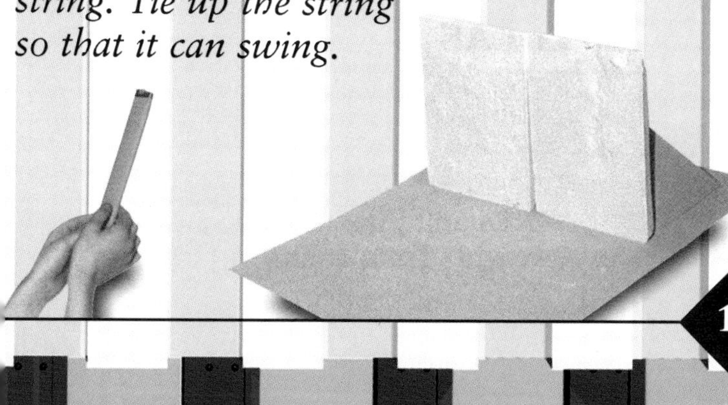

6 You will find that the block with the metal wire will last a lot longer before it shatters than the block without any wire.

NATURAL STRUCTURES

WHAT YOU NEED
Plastic tray
Large bowl
Jug of water
Modelling clay
Sand and soil
Green powder paint
Model trees
Saw

SOME OF THE LARGEST and most impressive structures found on this planet are not made by humans at all. Instead they have been formed naturally by the forces of the wind, sea, rivers or even by the movement of the massive plates of rock that make up the Earth's surface. These structures include soaring mountains, enormous canyons and towering waterfalls. This project shows you how a river can carve shapes and structures into the landscape.

FREEZING WATER

Water can change the shape of the land when it freezes. To see how, fill a plastic bottle with water. Screw the top on tightly. Put it in a sealed plastic bag in the freezer all night. The water expands as it freezes and shatters the plastic bottle.

7 Slowly pour in water at the back of the tray. Watch it flow down the slope, carving a path into the sand and soil. Make sure you catch the water in a bowl.

FLOWING RIVER

1 Ask an adult to saw off the front of a plastic tray.

2 Put some mounds of modelling clay around the bottom of the tray.

3 Pour the soil over the mounds so that they are covered. Make sure that the soil forms a slope from the back of the tray down to the open front.

4 Cover the soil with a layer of dry sand.

5 Now cover the sand with a layer of green powder paint to give a grass effect.

6 Add some model trees. Make a record of what it looks like by drawing or taking a photograph.

WHY IT WORKS

Water always flows down a slope (1). As it does so, it picks up soil particles and carries them along. The more soil it carries, the more it changes the landscape around it. Some rivers form huge bends called meanders (2). Over time, these bends are worn away, leaving small, crescent-shaped lakes called ox-bow lakes (3).

(3)

(2)

(1)

CHOOSING SHAPES

WHAT YOU NEED
Coloured card
Tracing paper
Scissors
Ruler
Pen
Hexagon stencil
Glue

OTHER PROJECTS IN THIS BOOK have shown you how to decide which material is the best for your structure Another thing that designers and engineers have to decide is the shape of the structure. This project shows how shapes that fit together exactly are good for covering an area. They also make strong structures

HEXAGON GAME

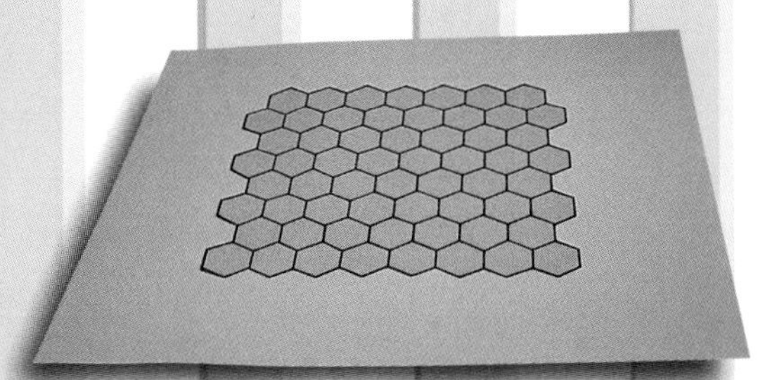

1 Using a stencil, draw and cut out 64 hexagonal (six-sided) shapes from two colours of card. Make sure they are all the same size.

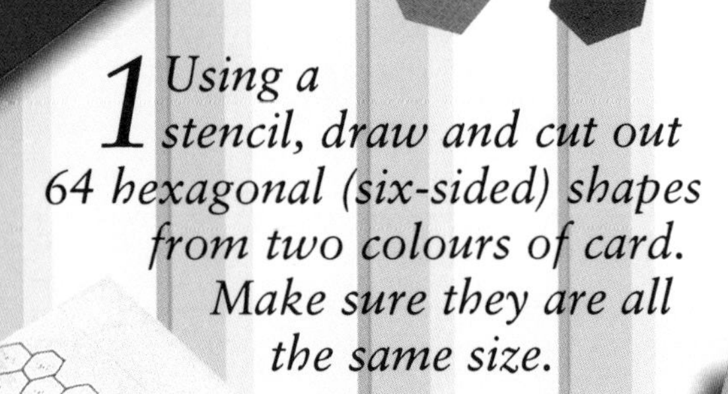

2 Now stencil onto a piece of card 64 hexagons which tessellate (fit together exactly). Trace the pattern and transfer it onto a sheet of coloured card.

3 Ask an adult to cut out both patterns and stick them together to make a strong grid. Go over the lines with a pen.

4 Stick your hexagon grid onto another, larger sheet of card.

5 Ask an adult to cut out this shape from card and fold it to make a small cube. Mark three sides with a 1 and the other three sides with a 2. This will be your game dice. Ask someone to play the hexagon game with you.

MAKE A MOSAIC

Using lots of different shapes and colours, make a pattern or picture on card. This type of picture is called a mosaic.

WHY IT WORKS

Hexagons can cover the board because they tessellate. This means that they fit together exactly without overlapping or leaving gaps. Shapes that tessellate make strong structures. Bees use hexagons to make a honeycomb.

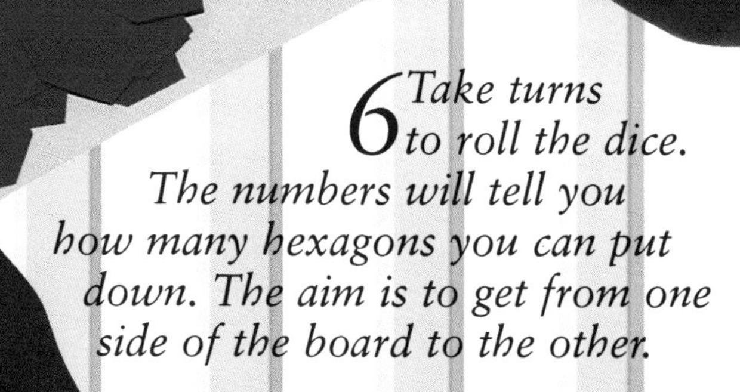

6 Take turns to roll the dice. The numbers will tell you how many hexagons you can put down. The aim is to get from one side of the board to the other.

*T*ESTING SHAPES

WHAT YOU NEED
Two identical cardboard tubes
Coins
Books
Plastic cups

YOU TESTED DIFFERENT TYPES of material for strength on pages 8-9. Strength is an important factor when deciding if the shape of a structure suits a task. Tessellating shapes are strong and are good for covering an area, as you saw in the last project. This project shows you how some shapes can be strong in one direction but very weak in another.

WHY IT WORKS

The shape of the tube means that it can take a lot of compressional (squeezing) force along its length. However, its sides are weak, and they will collapse when the slightest compressional force is applied there.

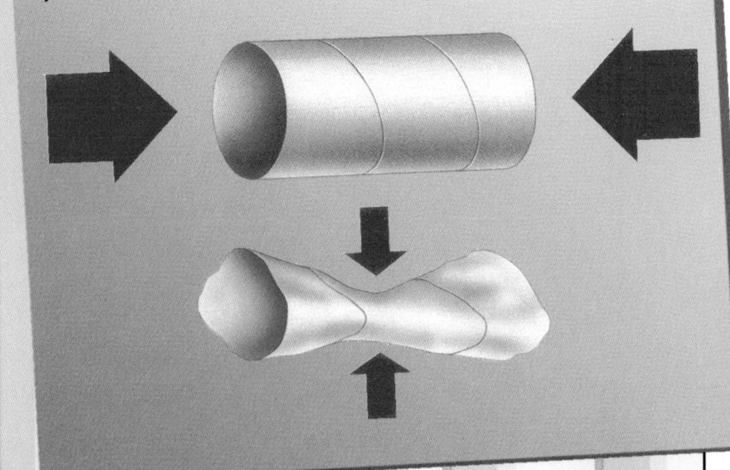

EGG STRENGTH

Repeat the project opposite, but this time use an egg instead of the tube. You will find that, like the tube, the egg can bear more weight when it is standing upright (you will need modelling clay to hold it in place) than when it is on its side.

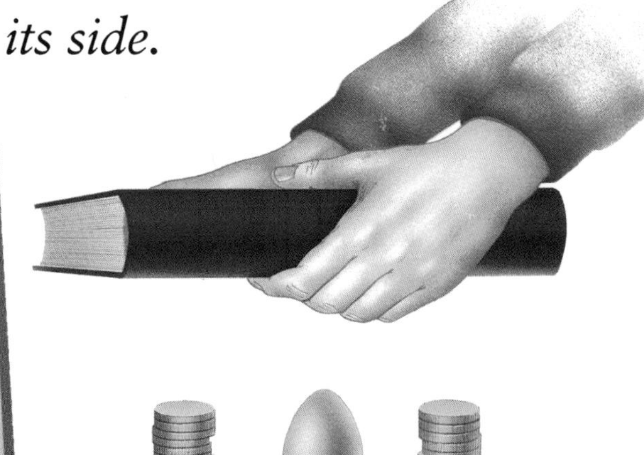

TUBE TESTING

1 Place a cardboard tube on its side. Stack coins on either side of the tube, until they are just below the width of the tube itself.

2 Start to balance books on top of the tube. Keep adding books until the tube collapses and the books rest on the stacks of coins.

3 Place the second tube on its end. Put plastic cups that are just smaller than the tube on either side.

4 Now repeat the project by placing books on top of the tube. See how many books have to be added before the tube collapses.

5 You will find that this time you need more books before the tube collapses.

TALL STRUCTURES

WHAT YOU NEED
Ruler
Pen
Thick card
Coloured card
Glue
Scissors

WHEN PUTTING TOGETHER A BUILDING, engineers and designers have to be aware of the stresses and forces that the building might be subjected to over its lifetime. They must then find the best materials and shapes to keep the building upright. This project shows you one solution for coping with the large forces a tall skyscraper has to put up with.

REACH FOR THE SKY

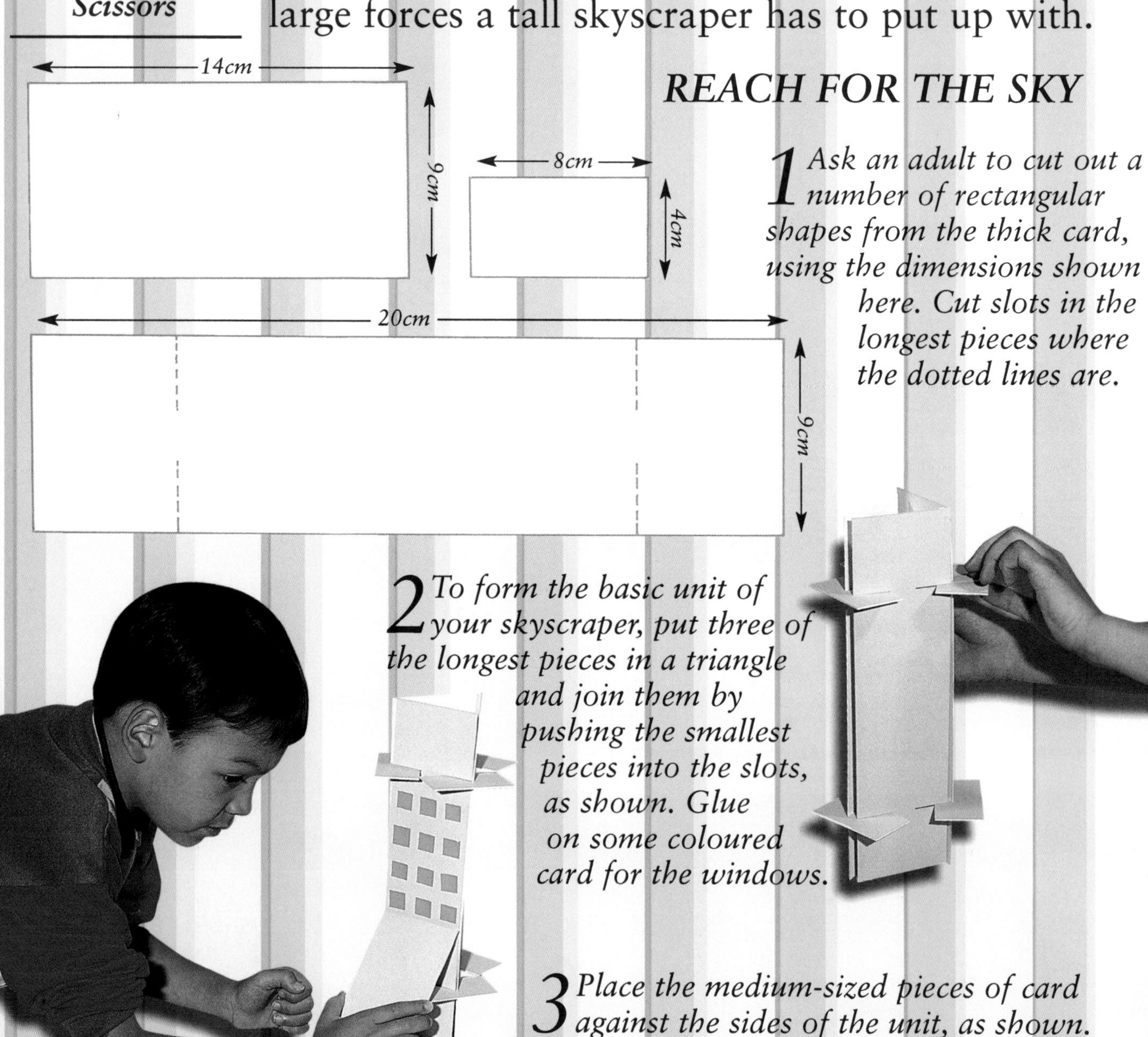

1 Ask an adult to cut out a number of rectangular shapes from the thick card, using the dimensions shown here. Cut slots in the longest pieces where the dotted lines are.

2 To form the basic unit of your skyscraper, put three of the longest pieces in a triangle and join them by pushing the smallest pieces into the slots, as shown. Glue on some coloured card for the windows.

3 Place the medium-sized pieces of card against the sides of the unit, as shown. Repeat step 2 to make lots of basic units.

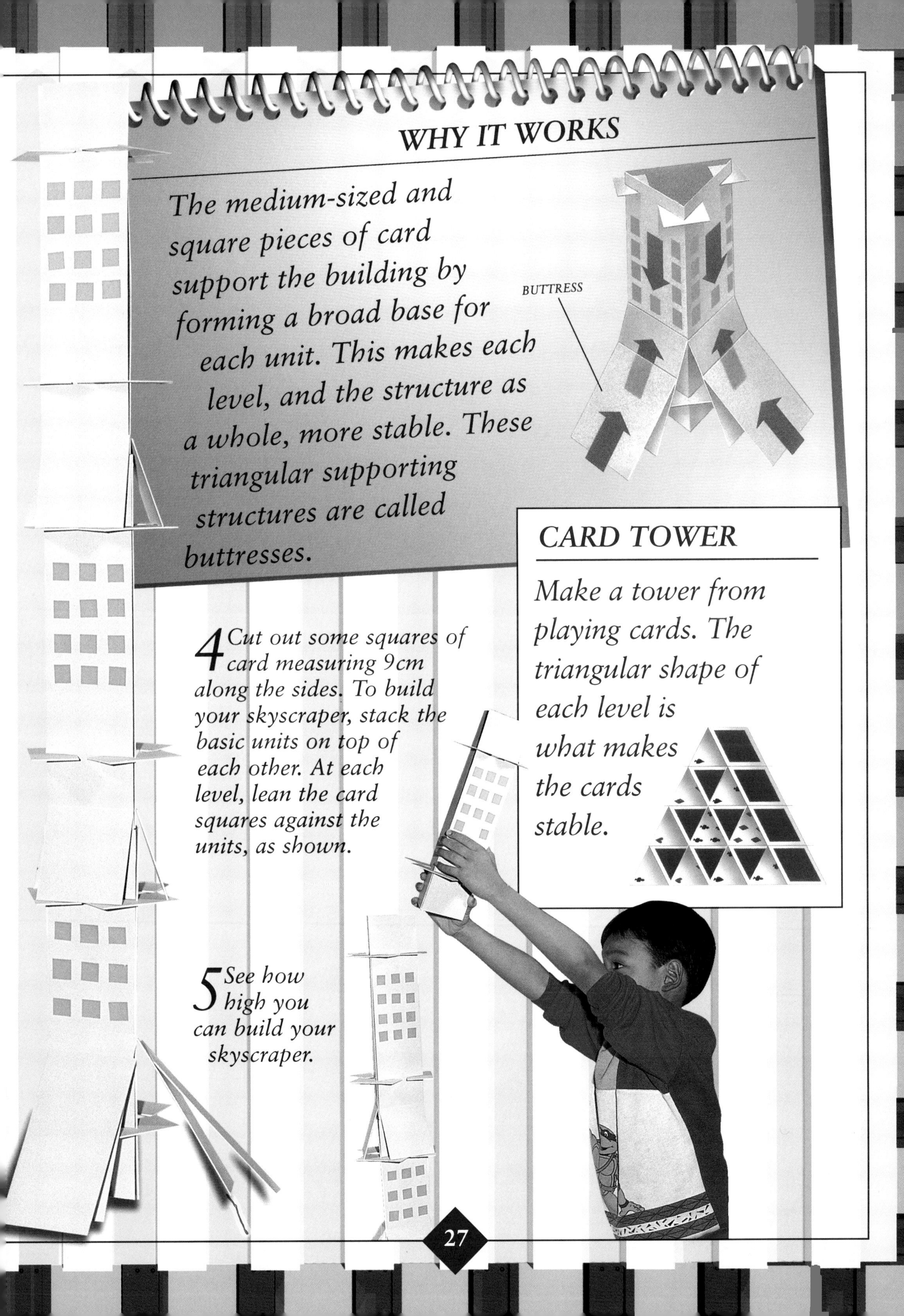

WHY IT WORKS

The medium-sized and square pieces of card support the building by forming a broad base for each unit. This makes each level, and the structure as a whole, more stable. These triangular supporting structures are called buttresses.

CARD TOWER

Make a tower from playing cards. The triangular shape of each level is what makes the cards stable.

4 Cut out some squares of card measuring 9cm along the sides. To build your skyscraper, stack the basic units on top of each other. At each level, lean the card squares against the units, as shown.

5 See how high you can build your skyscraper.

BUILDING BRIDGES

THE LAST PROJECT SHOWED you how to build upwards. But what happens if you have to build a structure that runs across something? Bridges give designers and engineers different problems. This project shows some of the ways that these problems can be overcome.

WHAT YOU NEED
Six wooden blocks
Pencils
Sticky tape
Thick card
String, Glue
Coloured card
Modelling clay

CANTILEVER BRIDGE

Another bridge structure is the cantilever bridge. Make your own cantilever bridge, as shown here, and see how much weight it can support.

BRIDGING THE GAP

1 Tape pencils to two corners of each wooden block, as shown here.

2 Ask an adult to cut out strips of thick card the same width as the wooden blocks. For the first bridge, simply place one strip between two of the blocks.

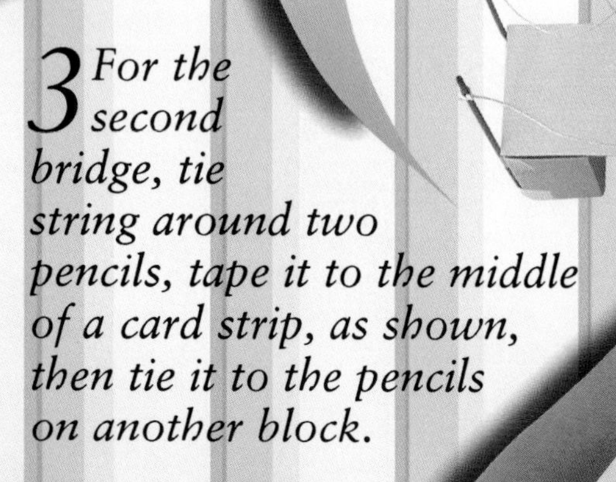

3 For the second bridge, tie string around two pencils, tape it to the middle of a card strip, as shown, then tie it to the pencils on another block.

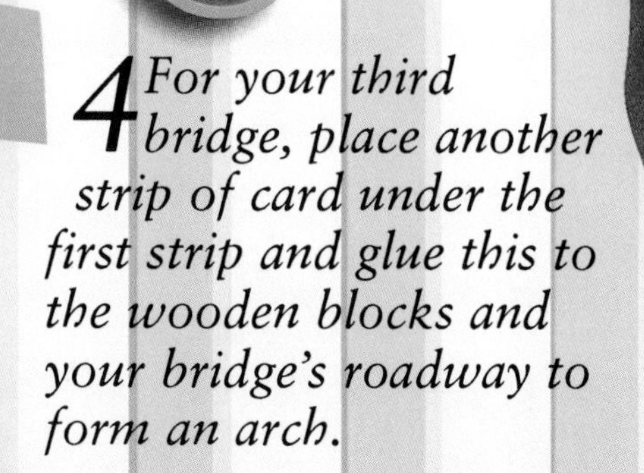

4 For your third bridge, place another strip of card under the first strip and glue this to the wooden blocks and your bridge's roadway to form an arch.

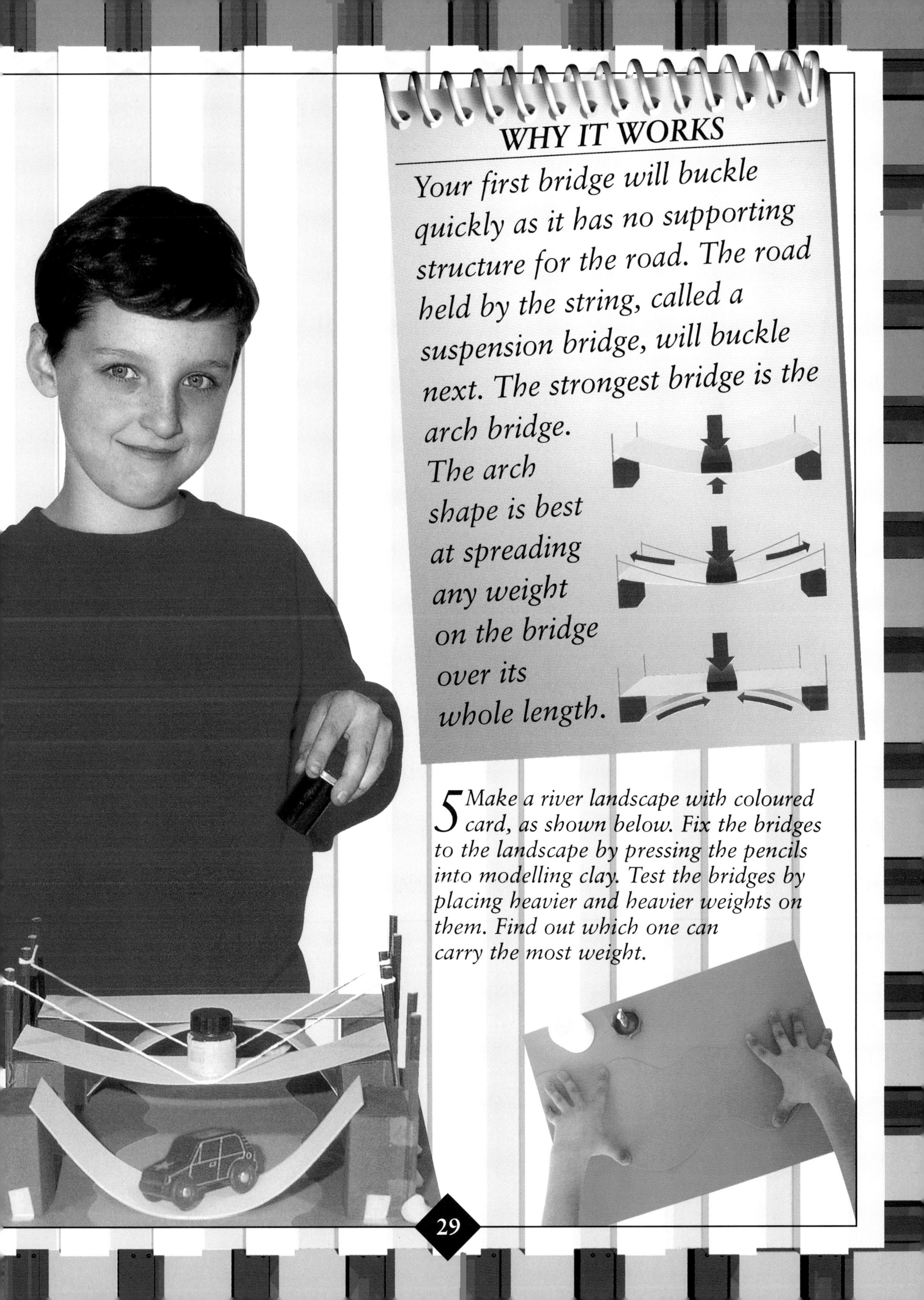

WHY IT WORKS

Your first bridge will buckle quickly as it has no supporting structure for the road. The road held by the string, called a suspension bridge, will buckle next. The strongest bridge is the arch bridge. The arch shape is best at spreading any weight on the bridge over its whole length.

5 Make a river landscape with coloured card, as shown below. Fix the bridges to the landscape by pressing the pencils into modelling clay. Test the bridges by placing heavier and heavier weights on them. Find out which one can carry the most weight.

*F*INDING OUT MORE

ARCH This is a natural or artificial structure which crosses an open area in a curve. *Find out how an arch can make a bridge stronger in the project on pages 28-29.*

COMPRESSIONAL FORCE This is a force which squeezes something. *See how you can test different objects against compressional force in the project on pages 24-25.*

ELASTIC When a material is elastic, it is capable of returning to its original shape after it has been squashed or pulled. *You can find out how to make metal wire elastic in the project on pages 10-11.*

PLASTIC A material is plastic if it can be shaped when it is soft and then sets hard into its new shape. *See how to make plastic material on pages 12-13.*

STRONG SILK

Some of the silk that spiders make, which they use to spin their webs, is actually stronger than steel of the same thickness.

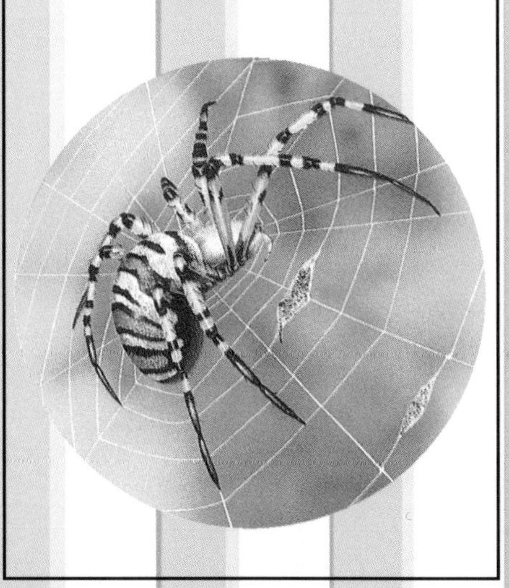

HOT STUFF

The tiles that cover the Space Shuttle are made from a material that can withstand the high temperatures of re-entering the Earth's atmosphere.

SKYSCRAPER This is a very tall building usually found in large cities. *Find out one way of keeping very tall buildings, such as skyscrapers, upright in the project on pages 26-27.*

INSIDE BONES

The bones in your body are not solid. Instead they are full of holes containing bone marrow and blood vessels. This means that they are strong as well as light.

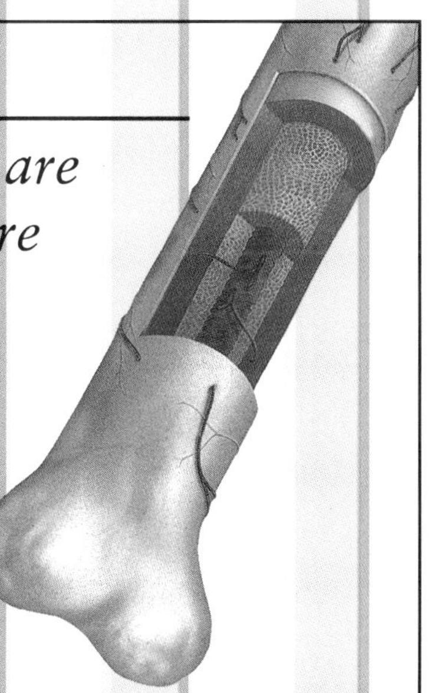

WARP THREADS

These are the threads that run up and down a material as it is being woven. *You can learn how to weave your own material on pages 16-17.*

SUSPENSION BRIDGE

This uses long cables hung from towers at either end of the bridge to help it take the weight of objects crossing it. *Build your own suspension bridge in the project on pages 28-29.*

TESSELLATE

When shapes tessellate, they cover an area completely without overlapping or leaving any gaps. *Find out on pages 22-23 how you can use tessellating shapes to make a fun game to play.*

WEFT THREADS

These are the threads that run across a material. *See how weaving weft threads through warp threads on a loom can make a material in the project on pages 16-17.*

CONCORDE

The windscreen of Concorde is covered in a very thin sheet of solid gold. This is because gold is very good at protecting the jetliner from the heat that is generated when it flies faster than the speed of sound.

INDEX